KU-715-759

DATA INTERPRETATION
FOR THE
MRCP

DATA INTERPRETATION FOR THE MRCP

Peter Clark BSc MBChB MRCP(UK)
Career Registrar in Haematology
Western Infirmary
Glasgow

Roderick Neilson MBChB MRCP(UK) Dip.RCPath
Senior Registrar in Haematology
The Royal Infirmary
Glasgow

© 1994 PASTEST
Egerton Court, Parkgate Estate
Knutsford, Cheshire
WA16 8DX
Tel: (01565) 755226

All rights reserved. No part of this publication may be reproduced, stored
in a retrieval system, or transmitted, in any form or by any means,
electronic, mechanical, photocopying, recording or otherwise without
prior permission of the publishers.

First published 1994
Reprinted 1995
Reprinted 1996

ISBN 0 906896 81 9

A catalogue record for this book is available from the British Library.

The information contained within this book was obtained by PasTest from
reliable sources. However, while every effort has been made to ensure its
accuracy, no responsibility for loss, damage or injury occasioned to any
person acting or refraining from action as a result of information contained
herein can be accepted by the publishers or authors.

Text prepared by Turner Associates, Congleton, Cheshire.
Printed and bound by Biddles Ltd, Guildford, Surrey.

CONTENTS

Other PasTest Titles for MRCP Part 2

MRCP Part 2 Revision Book (Second Edition)
 Eva Lester   *0 906896 76 2*

MRCP Part 2 Preparation for the Clinical Examination
 Julian Gray   *0 906896 45 2*

MRCP 2 Paediatric Practice Exams: Case Histories & Data Interpretations
 Deb Pal & Paul Gringras *0 906896 62 2*

MRCP Part 2 Pocket Books
 Richard Hawkins

Bk 1: Cardiology and Respiratory Medicine	*0 906896 37 1*
Bk 2: Gastroenterology, Endocrinology and Renal	*0 906896 42 8*
Bk 3: Haematology, Rheumatology and Neurology	*0 906896 47 9*

For further details telephone PasTest on 01565 755226.

PasTest Intensive Courses for MRCP

The following courses are available from PasTest:

MRCP 1 General Medicine (6 consecutive days and weekend courses)
MRCP 1 Paediatrics (6 consecutive days and weekend courses)
MRCP 2 General Medicine Written (4 day and weekend courses)
MRCP 2 General Medicine Written Mock Exam (weekend courses)
MRCP 2 General Medicine Clinicals (4 day courses)
MRCP 2 General Medicine Clinical Technique (weekend courses)
MRCP 2 Paediatrics Written Paper (4 day courses)
MRCP 2 Paediatrics Clinical (4 day and weekend courses)

For full details contact:
**PasTest, Dept. DI, Egerton Court, Parkgate Estate,
Knutsford, Cheshire, WA16 8DX
Tel: 01565 755226 Fax: 01565 650264**

FOREWORD

The written part of the MRCP Part 2 examination comprises three sections: case histories ('grey cases'), photographs and data interpretation. The latter is designed to test the candidate's ability to arrive at a reasonable diagnosis from a set of data and is intended to replicate the day to day decision-making faced by all doctors working in general medicine.

The data interpretation paper consists of ten questions which must be answered within forty-five minutes. Questions include electrocardiographs, echocardiograms, cardiac catheter studies, 'specialised' data such as family pedigrees audiograms, biochemistry, haematology and pulmonary function tests.

Questions asked fall into three main groups: "What is the diagnosis?", "List the abnormalities present", and "Suggest a number of tests which will assist in attaining a diagnosis". It should be realised that in a number of questions there will be more than one answer and that marks are given on a sliding scale; the highest marks are awarded to the most appropriate answer, other answers are given lesser credit.

In our opinion, success in the written part of the MRCP depends not only on a firm knowledge of general medicine but also on frequent practice at the type of questions that may be asked. We have found, as have the majority of our colleagues, that the more mock examinations and practice papers attempted, the greater the likelihood of passing the exam.

This book contains ten well balanced papers, with answers and explanations of the answers given. It is not a textbook of medicine but is designed to allow the reader to gain experience of the type of questions asked in postgraduate medical exams and to identify any gaps in knowledge for those sitting the MRCP. To this end we have included a list of common differential diagnoses at the beginning of the book. Although not comprehensive, we hope that it will prove useful in final revision for the MRCP.

We have tried to ensure that our explanations are in keeping with current thinking, and we hope that our own bias has been kept to a minimum.

DEDICATION

This book is dedicated to R.L.C., C.A.C. and B.J.R.

ACKNOWLEDGEMENTS

Our thanks to Dr. C.A. Leslie for suggestions and proof reading and to R.M. Leslie for provision of audiogram material.

NORMAL RANGES

SERUM	NORMAL RANGE
Albumin	36-52 g/l
Amylase	70-300 iu/l
Bicarbonate	22-28 mmol/l
Bilirubin	5-20 μmol/l
Calcium	2.20-2.60 mmol/l
Chloride	95-105 mmol/l
Creatine kinase	23-175 iu/l
Creatinine	60-120 μmol/l
Gammaglutaryltransferase (GGT)	< 40 iu/l
Globulins	24-37 g/l
Immunoglobulins	
IgG	5.3-16.5 g/l
IgA	0.8-4.0 g/l
IgM	0.5-2.0 g/l
Iron	14-29 μmol/l
Iron binding capacity (TIBC)	45-75 μmol/l
Lactate dehydrogenase (LDH)	100-300 iu/l
Magnesium	0.70-1.00 mmol/l
Osmolality	270-295 mmol/l
Phophatase (acid)	0-4 iu/l
Phophatase (alkaline)	40-115 iu/l
Phosphate	0.8-1.4 mmol/l
Potassium	3.5-5.0 mmol/l
Protein	62-82 g/l
Sodium	135-145 mmol/l
Thyroid function tests	
T_4	54-144 nmol/l
TSH	0.10-5.0 mU/l
T_3	0.8-2.7 nmol/l
FT_4	9-25 pmol/l
TBG	10-30 mg/l
Transaminase ALT	11-55 iu/l
Transaminase AST	13-42 iu/l
Transferrin	2-4 g/l
Urate	0.24-0.45 mmol/l
Urea	2.5-6.6 mmol/l

Normal Ranges

PLASMA   NORMAL RANGE

Glucose   3.0-5.9 mmol/l
Arterial blood gases
    $[H^+]$ 36-43 nmol/l
    pCO_2 4.6-6.0 kPa
    $[HCO3^-]$ 20-28 mmol/l
    pO_2 10.5-13.5 kPa
Lactate   0.63-2.44 mmol/l
Pyruvate   34-80 μmol/l

CEREBROSPINAL FLUID (CSF)

Glucose   2.5-3.9 mmol/l
Protein   <0.45 g/l

URINE

Catecholamines   <1.3 μmol/24 hrs
VMA (HMMA)   9-36 μmol/24 hrs
5HIAA   10-50 μmol/24 hrs
Microalbumin   <30 mg/l
Creatinine clearance   60-110 ml/min

MISCELLANEOUS

Faecal fat   <18 mmol/24 hrs
Xylose excretion test
    Urine excretion (25 g dose)   >33 mmol/5 hrs
    Urine excretion (5 g dose)   >8 mmol/5 hrs
    Blood xylose at 1 hr (25 g dose)   2.0-4.8 mmol/l
    Blood xylose at 2 hrs (25 g dose)   1.0-5.0 mmol/l

DIFFERENTIAL DIAGNOSES

During our own preparation for the MRCP, we realised that the key to a substantial number of data questions lay in being familiar with the core element of the question. Many questions are built around the same data but appear unfamiliar because of the way in which the case is presented. Following recognition of these basic data 'patterns' the candidate is required to interpret the data in light of the history given. To facilitate this, the following chapter contains a list of the basic data patterns used in this book, accompanied by the common clinical diagnoses with which they are associated. They are arranged in alphabetical order.

We hope that these differential diagnoses, although not comprehensive, will assist the candidate's understanding of the data and will provide an aide memoire in the final preparation for the MRCP examination.

ACID/BASE:

pH	pCO2	Bicarbonate	
↓	⬄	↓	Metbolic Acidosis
↓	↑	⬄/↑	Respiratory Acidosis
↑	⬄	↑	Metabolic Alkalosis
↑	↓	⬄/↑	Respiratory Alkalosis
			Compensated/Chronic
⬄	↓	↓	Metabolic Acidosis
⬄	↑	↑ ↑	Respiratory Acidosis
↑	⬄/↑	↑ ↑	Metabolic Alkalosis
⬄	↓	↓ ↓	Respiratory Alkalosis

BLOOD FILM:

Causes of a leucoerythroblastic anaemia include:
    Metastatic involvement of the marrow by carcinoma
    (commonly prostatic, breast and lung)
    Myelofibrosis
    Myeloma
    Severe haemorrhage or haemolysis

BLOOD VOLUME:

Interpretation

Disease	RBC volume	Plasma volume
Stress Diuretics Dehydration Oedema Altitude	Normal	Low
Cirrhosis Nephritis CCF Myeloma Waldenstroms	Normal/low	High
Anaemia	Low	Normal
Polycythaemia	High	Normal

CEREBROSPINAL FLUID EXAMINATION:

Below are some of the major features of CSF examination which may assist in the formulation of a diagnosis.

Protein	Colour	Turbidity	Glucose	Cells	Aetiology
↑ ↑ ↑	Yellow	↑ /-			Tumour
↑ ↑	pus	↑ ↑	↓ ↓	↑ ↑	Bacterial meningitis
↑	clear	↑ /-	↓	Mixed cells	Tuberculous meningitis
-	yellow	-	-	-	Jaundice
↑ ↑	red blood		-	r.b.c.	S.A.H.
↑	red blood on 1st sample			r.b.c.	Traumatic tap
-		-	↓ ↓	-	Hypoglycaemia

Key to Diagram
↑ ↑ ↑ = Very High
↑ ↑ = High
↑ = Moderately raised
↓ ↓ = Very Low
↓ = Low
↑ /- = Raised or Normal
- = Normal

COAGULATION:

Disseminated intravascular coagulation common causes:

Infection:	Bacterial (Gram -ve Sepsis)
	Viral
Obstetric:	Septic abortion
	Eclampsia
	Amniotic fluid embolus
	Ante partum haemorrhage
Malignancy:	Disseminated carcinomatosis
	Leukaemia

COLD HAEMAGGLUTININS:

Aetiology

Idiopathic
Associated with infections - Mycoplasma
                           - Infectious mononucleosis
Associated with lymphoproliferative disorders
Paroxysmal cold haemoglobinuria

CYTOCHEMISTRY:

In leukaemia

AML	M1	M2	M3	M4	M5	M6	M7
Peroxidase Sudan Black	+	+	+	+	+	-	-
Esterases	-	+/-	+/-	+ +	+ +	+/-	+/-
PAS	-	+	+	+	+ +	+	+/-

ALL	common ALL	B cell ALL	T cell ALL
Peroxidase Sudan Black	-	-	-
Esterases	-	-	-
PAS	+/-	+/-	+/-
Acid Phosp	-/+	-/+	+ +

DEXAMETHASONE SUPPRESSION:

Conditions with excess cortisol

Aetiology	*Cx Plasma*	*Cx Urine*	*2 mg Dex*	*8 mg Dex*	*ACTH*
Pituitary Driven	N/High	High	No Supp	Supp	N/High
Ectopic ACTH	High	V High	No Supp	No Supp	V High
Adrenal Carcinoma	High	V High	No Supp	No Supp	Low
Adrenal Adenoma	N/High	High	No Supp	No Supp	Low

Key
Cx   = Cortisol
Dex = Dexamethasone
Supp = Suppression

DIMORPHIC BLOOD FILM:

Causes
       Iron deficiency anaemia on treatment
       Sideroblastic anaemia
       Combined deficiency of folate and iron
       Transfusion of patients with microcytosis or macrocytosis.

ELECTROCARDIOGRAPH:

a) HYPERKALAEMIA

The ECG changes seen in hyperkalaemia are:
  Tented T waves
  Diminution or absence of P waves
  Broad complex ventricular rhythm (sine wave)
  Slurring of the ST segment
  Asystole

b) VENTRICULAR TACHYCARDIA

The features which may assist in the diagnosis of ventricular tachycardia.
  The presence of left axis deviation
  Slight variation in heart rate
  Changing conduction patterns including the presence of fusion and
  capture beats
  A-V dissociation

ERYTHROPOIETIN:

Inappropriate secretion

Conditions where inappropriate secretion of erythropoeitin leads to a
secondary polycythaemia:
  Hypernephroma (renal carcinoma)
  Hepatoma
  Cerebellar haemangioma
  Uterine fibroid

GENETICS:

Some autosomal dominant conditions
    Familial hypercholesterolaemia
    Neurofibromatosis
    Polyposis coli

Some autosomal recessive conditions
    Cystic fibrosis
    Phenylketonuria
    Spinal muscle atrophy

Some X-linked recessive conditions
    Haemophilia A
    Red-green colourblindness
    Duchenne muscular dystrophy

HYPERCHLORAEMIC ACIDOSIS:

A differential diagnosis of normal anion gap acidosis includes:
    Carbonic anhydrase inhibitors:acetazolamide therapy
    Renal tubular acidosis
    Ammonium chloride administration
    Ureteric transplantation

HYPERPARATHYROIDISM:

The differential diagnosis of the common biochemical changes associated with increased parathormone levels.

Hyper - Parathyroidism	Calcium	Phosphate	Serum Alkaline Phosphatase
Primary	↑	↓ /-	-/ ↑
Primary (renal impairment)	-	-	-/ ↑
Ectopic	↑	↓	↑ ↑
Secondary	↓ /-	↓	↑
Secondary (renal impairment)	↓ /-	↑	↑
Tertiary	↑	↓ /-	↑ ↑

Key to Diagram

↑ ↑ ↑ = Very High
↑ ↑   = High
↑   = Moderately raised
↓ ↓   = Very Low
↓   = Low
↑ /-   = Raised or Normal
  -    = Normal

HYPOSPLENISM:

Causes

Congenital – Splenic atrophy:
     Sickle cell disease
     Coeliac disease
     Crohn's disease
     Ulcerative colitis
     Essential thrombocythaemia
     Fanconi's anaemia

IRON:

Serum levels, and total binding capacity

Interpretation of serum iron/total iron binding capacity (TIBC).

	Iron Deficiency	*Chronic Infection/ Malignancy*	*Thalassaemias*	*Haemochromatosis*
Serum iron	↓	↓	N	↑
TIBC	↑	↓	N	N
%Sat^n	↓	N	N	↑

<u>Key</u>
% Sat^n = percentage saturation
↑ = increased
↓ = decreased

LIPOPROTEINS:

Electrophoresis

Lipoprotein abnormalities and the major clinical syndromes associated
with hyperplipidaemia.

Primary lipid	Abnormal lipoprotein	Freidrickson classification	Clinical presentation
Triglyceride	Ochylomicrons	I	Familial hyperchylomicron
Cholesterol	LDL(β)	IIa	Familial/Polygenic hypercholesterol Familial combined hyperlipidaemia
Cholesterol Triglyceride	LDL(β) VLDL(preβ)	IIb	Familial combined hyperlipidaemia
Cholesterol Triglyceride	IDL(β)	III	Broad beta disease
Triglyceride	VLDL(preβ)	IV	Familial hypertriglyceride
			Familial combined hyperlipidaemia
Triglyceride	VLDL(preβ) Chylomicrons	V	Familial combined hyperlipidaemia

MONOSPOT:

Positive monospot tests are found in association with:
   glandular fever
   lymphoma
   hepatitis

PANCYTOPENIA:

With raised reticulocyte count

Infiltration of or toxic insult to bone marrow
Systemic lupus erythematosus associated haemolytic anaemia
Paroxysmal nocturnal haemoglobinuria
Aplastic anaemia

PORPHYRIA:

	Urine dALA/PBG	Urine porphyrins	Faeces porphyrins
Associated with neurological disturbance in acute attacks:			
Porphyria variegata	- (+)	- (+)	+ (+)
Hereditary coproporphyria	- (+)	- (+)	+ (+)
Not associated with neurological manifestations			
Cutaneous hepatic porphyria	-	+	-
Congenital erythropoetic porphyria	-	+	+
Erythrohepatic porphyria	-	-	+

Figures in brackets indicate acute attacks. Hereditary coproporphyria is rarely associated with skin lesions.

PROTEIN:

Serum electrophoresis patterns

Albumin	Globulins α1	α2	β	Gamma	
↓					Any illness
↓	↑	↑	-	-	Acute phase
↓	-	-	-	↑	Autoimmune
↓	↓	-	β-Gamma fusion	↑	Cirrhosis
↓	↓	↑	-	↓	Nephrotic

PSEUDOHYPERKALAEMIA:

Causes
    Acute myeloproliferative disorders
    Chronic myeloproliferative disorders
    Chronic lymphatic leukaemia
    Rheumatoid arthritis

PARTIAL THROMBOPLASTIN TIME:

Causes of prolongation
    Newborn
    Liver disease
    Haemophilia
    Consumptive coagulopathy
    Defibrination
    Anticoagulants
    Specimen insufficient in volume or contaminated with anticoagulant
    The presence of a lupus anticoagulant

PARTIAL THROMBOPLASTIN TIME:

Causes of shortening
    Pregnancy
    Post partum
    Exercise
    Post surgical
    Oestrogen administration
    Recent deep venous thrombosis
    Pulmonary thromboembolism
    Difficulty or delay in venepuncture

PULMONARY FUNCTION TESTS:

FEV_1	FVC	FEV1/FVC	KCO	TLC	RV	Diagnosis
↓↓	↔/↓	< 70%	↔/↑	↑	↑↑	Asthma
↓↓	↔/↓	< 70%	↓	↔	↑↑	Bronchitis
↓↓	↔/↓	< 70%	↓↓	↑↑	↑↑	Emphysema
↓↓	↓	> 70%	↓↓	↓↓	↓	Interstitial disease

PUNCTATE BASOPHILIA:
Causes
    Heavy metal poisoning (lead, zinc, mercury)
    Beta thalassaemia trait
    Liver disease
    Myelodysplastic states
    Haemolytic anaemia

RED CELL:

Causes of oxidative haemolysis:
    Salazopyrin
    Dapsone
    Maloprim
    Nitrates and nitrites

SODIUM:

a) **Hypernatraemia/hyperosmolar conditions**

    Water depletion/insufficient action by ADH to retain water:
        Diabetes insipidus
        Diabetes mellitus with an osmotic diuresis
        Therapeutic osmotic diuresis
    Loss of thirst mechanism: Unconscious patient
    Excessive salt intake

b) **Hyponatraemia/Hypo-osmolar conditions**

    Sodium loss with inappropriate fluid replacement:
        vomiting
        diarrhoea
        fever
    Syndrome of inappropriate ADH secretion.
    Addison's disease (late).
    Secondary hyperaldosteronism in oedema.

THALASSAEMIA:

α-thalassaemia	Heterozygote	Homozygote	Defect
α-thal-1	Thalassaemia minor 5-10% Hb Barts at birth	Hydrops foetalis 80% Hb Barts	Deletion of 2 α-globin genes
α-thal-2	Thalassaemia minor 1-2% Hb Barts at birth	Thalassaemia minor 5-10% Hb Barts at birth	Deletion of 1 α-globin gene

β-thalassaemia	Heterozygote	Homozygote
	Thalassaemia minor 3-6% HbA$_2$	Thalassaemia major 98% HbF 2% HbA$_2$

Defects causing impaired β-globin synthesis.
    Gene deletion
    RNA transcriptional mutations
    RNA processing mutations
    Production of non-functional RNA

THYROID BINDING GLOBULIN:

Causes of a reduced TBG
Nephrotic syndrome
Congenital deficiency of TBG

Causes of a raised TBG
Pregnancy
Newborn
Use of the combined oral contraceptive pill

THYROID FUNCTION TESTS:

	TT4	FT4	TSH	TRH	T3
Hyperthyroidism	↑	↑	↓	0	
Hypothyroidism	↓	↓	↑	↑ ↑	
	↓	↓	↓	↑ or ↓	
T3 Thyrotoxicosis	N	N	↓	0	↑
↑ TBG	↑	N	N	N	
↓ TBG	↓	N	N	N	

<u>Key</u>
TT4 = Total T4   FT4 = Free T4
T3 = Tri-iodothyronine   TSH = Thyroid stimulating hormone
TRH = TSH response to TRH
↓ = decreased   ↑ = increased
N = normal levels   0 = No response
↑ or ↓ = hypothyroidism due to hypothalamic dysfunction is associated
with an increased TSH response to TRH.
Hypothyroidism due to pituitary dysfunction is associated with a
reduced response.

WATER DEPRIVATION TESTS:

The table below shows the results of urine testing of osmolality and the response of urine and serum osmolality to a standard water deprivation test.

| | *U osm* | Water deprivation | | |
		U osm	*S osm*	*+ DDAVP*
Nephrogenic D.I.	low	no ↑	↑	no ↑
Cranial D.I.	low	no ↑	↑	↑
Water intoxication	low	↑	↑	

Key
U osm   = Urine osmolality
S osm   = Serum osmolality
+ DDAVP   = the response of urine osmolality to an injection of DDAVP
↑   = increase

N.B. The water deprivation in subjects suspected of water intoxication has been carried out after a period of water restriction.

DATA INTERPRETATION PAPER 1

1. Time available: 45 minutes.

2. Answer **all 10 of the following questions** in the spaces provided.

3. When asked (for example) to list 3 diagnoses or investigations, one line will be provided for each answer. If more than the required number of answers are given, the additional answers will not be scored.

4. Go over your answers until the 45 minutes are up. You can then check your answers against the correct answers and teaching notes for this paper as given on page 133 onwards.

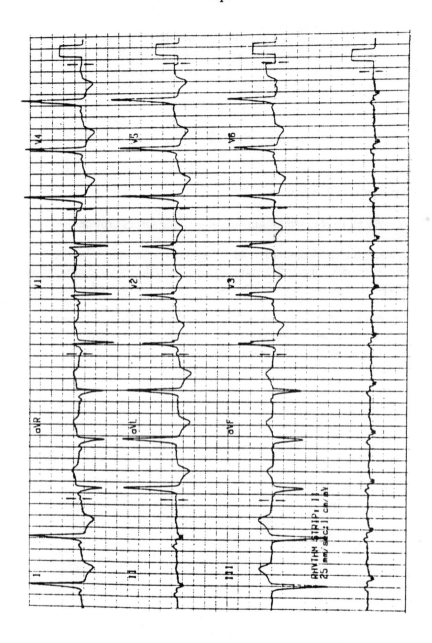

Figure 1

1.1

The ECG shown opposite (Fig. 1) is of a 24 year old lady who presented to her General Practitioner with 'panic attacks'.

a) What is the electrocardiographic diagnosis?

   ....

b) What further investigations are indicated?

   ....

   ....

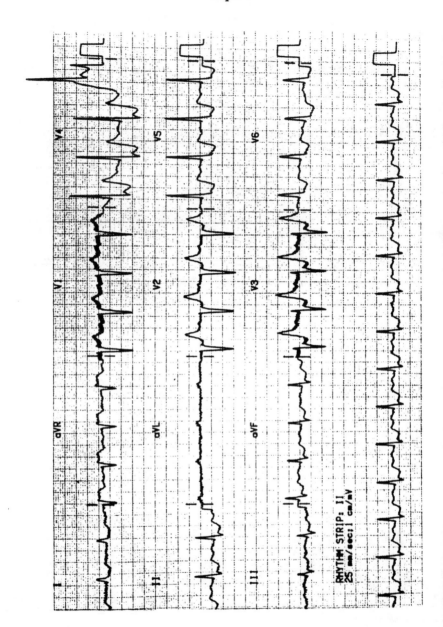

Figure 2

1.2

Creatine kinase at the time of ECG: 500 iu/l.

a) What diagnosis can be made from the ECG shown opposite (Fig. 2) taken ten hours after the occurrence of chest pain?

....

1.3

A 35 year old, known to have a chronically low serum calcium, was seen at a medical outpatient clinic.

Below are some results from this clinic

Ca^{++}	1.71 mmol/l
Albumin	42 g/l
Globulin	21 g/l
PTH	< 0.02 IU/l
Alkaline phosphatase	75 IU/l

He underwent treatment with calcium supplements and daily oral 1-α calcidol. At two month review his results were as follows:

Ca^{++}	2.12 mmol/l
Albumin	42 g/l
Total protein	66 g/l
Phosphate	1.08 mmol/l
Alkaline phosphatase	79 IU/l

a) What diagnosis is likely from his presenting biochemistry?

....

....

b) What are the possible causes of his review results?

....

....

c) What further investigations would be useful?

....

....

1.4

The protein electrophoresis shown below is taken from a patient with
hyperlipidaemia.

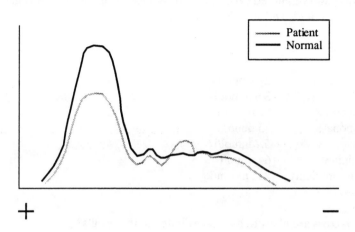

a) What diagnosis can be made?

....

1.5

A 65 year old non-insulin dependent diabetic, controlled on oral medication, was admitted unconscious after a road traffic accident.

His biochemistry was noted to be normal on admission and he was managed on intravenous fluids and soluble insulin.

Day 3

Na	125 mmol/l
K	3.6 mmol/l
Cl	92 mmol/l
Bicarbonate	25 mmol/l
Urea	5.2 mmol/l
Creatinine	64 μmol/l
Serum osmolality	268 mosm/kg

a) What factors are likely to have contributed to the results?

....

....

b) What other investigations should be carried out at initial presentation?

....

....

1.6

A sixty eight year old man presents with malaise, dyspnoea and angina. Physical examination is unremarkable. Examination of his blood shows the following:

Hb	6.4 g/dl
WBC	$38 \times 10^9/l$
Lymph	$31.8 \times 10^9/l$
Neut	$5.5 \times 10^9/l$
Eosin	$0.4 \times 10^9/l$
Baso	$0.3 \times 10^9/l$
Platelets	$178 \times 10^9/l$
MCV	84 fl

Film   Red cells normochromic with polychromasia and microspherocytes. Smear cells a prominent feature.

a) What are the two diagnoses?

....

....

b) What 3 other tests would you perform?

....

....

....

1.7

A 37 year old woman is found to have an MCV of 112 fl and a B_{12} level of 140 pmol/l. The following are the results of her Schilling Test:

Stage 1

	% of dose excreted at 24 hrs	Urine Vol in 24 hrs
^{58}Co-B_{12} orally	4%	1280 ml

Stage 2

^{58}Co-B_{12} + Intrinsic factor	4.3%	1330 ml

a) What is the likely cause of the macrocytosis?

....

1.8

The following are the results of examination of the cerebrospinal fluid of a 51 year old who presented with sudden onset of paraplegia. It was noted that the CSF tended to clot spontaneously on withdrawal:

CSF:
Pressure   18 cm H_2O
Protein   4.5 g/l
Xanthochromia + +
                  Non turbid

a) What is the cause of the above changes?

....

b) Can you suggest why the CSF tends to clot spontaneously?

....

1.9

The following laboratory results are from a 34 year old man being investigated for abdominal pain, mild arthralgia and a rash:

Hb	10.8 g/dl	Na	144 mmol/l
WBC	$8 \times 10^9/l$	K	4.7 mmol/l
Platelets	$412 \times 10^9/l$	Cl	108 mmol/l

Film	Normochromic	Bic	14 mmol/l
	Normocytic	Urea	18 mmol/l
	Eosinophilia	Creatinine	189 μmol/l
ESR	85 mm/1 hr	Glucose	4.8 mmol/l

Bilirubin	8 μmol/l
Alk Phos	115 IU/l
AST	12 IU/l
ALT	42 IU/l
LDH	308 IU/l

Rheum Factor   -ve
Anti Nuclear Factor   -ve
HbsAg   +ve

Urinalysis: Protein + +
              Blood +

a) What is the diagnosis?

....

b) What two other investigations should be performed?

....

....

1.10

A forty seven year old lady presents to Casualty with a right cerebrovascular accident. Her BP one week after admission was noted to be 170/122 mm Hg.

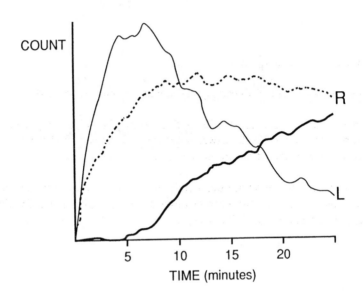

The graph shown represents the results of an isotope renogram carried out after initiation of antihypertensive medication.

a) What is the likely cause of her hypertension?

....

DATA INTERPRETATION PAPER 2

1. Time available: 45 minutes.

2. Answer **all 10 of the following questions** in the spaces provided.

3. When asked (for example) to list 3 diagnoses or investigations, one line will be provided for each answer. If more than the required number of answers are given, the additional answers will not be scored.

4. Go over your answers until the 45 minutes are up. You can then check your answers against the correct answers and teaching notes for this paper as given on page 138 onwards.

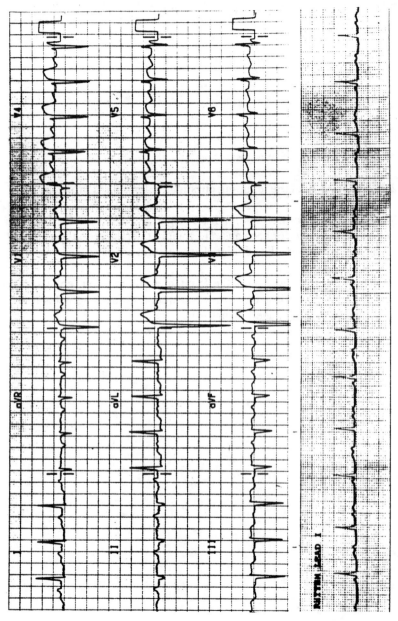

Figure 3

2.1

The ECG shown opposite (Fig. 3) is from a sixty two year old man who presented with chest pain.

a) What is the likely cause of his chest pain?

    ....

b) What complication has occurred?

    ....

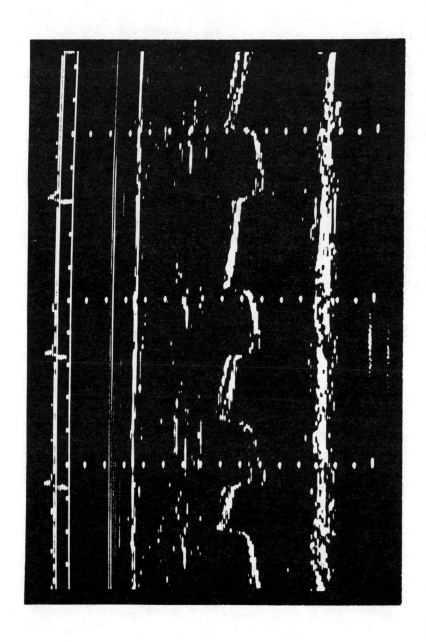

Figure 4

2.2

a) What two diagnoses can be made from the echocardiogram shown opposite (Fig. 4)?

....

....

2.3

A 62 year old man presents with long standing dyspnoea. Below is his admission biochemistry:

Na	128 mmol/l
K	5.4 mmol/l
Cl	88 mmol/l
Bic	32 mmol/l
Urea	10.4 mmol/l

a) Give a likely explanation for the biochemical upset?

....

b) He is oedema free. What is his overall sodium balance?

....

2.4

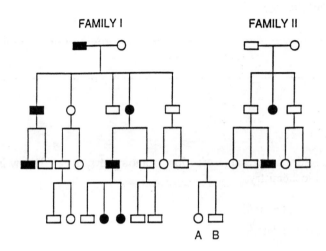

�■ = AFFECTED MALE
☐ = NORMAL MALE
● = AFFECTED FEMALE
○ = NORMAL FEMALE

a) What mode of inheritance is shown in family 'I'?

....

b) What mode of inheritance is shown in family 'II'?

....

2.5

A 22 year old man presents with tiredness 3 weeks after a severe upper respiratory tract infection.

Hb	9.2 g/dl
MCV	98 fl
MCH	29 g/dl
WBC	$8.3 \times 10^9/l$
Platelets	$218 \times 10^9/l$
Reticulocytes	8%
Monospot	Negative
Blood Film	Polychromasia, autoagglutination
	Occasional microspherocytes

a) What is the diagnosis?

   ....

2.6

A thirty year old man, diagnosed as having haemophilia A, presents with an early haemarthrosis of his right knee. His coagulation screen on admission is as follows:

Prothrombin time	16 s (Control 16 s)
Partial thromboplastin time	80 s (Control 35 s)
Thrombin time	9 s (Control 9 s)
Platelet count	$218 \times 10^9/l$
Factor VIII assay	< 2 IU/l

After treatment with Factor VIII concentrate, in standard calculated dosage, his coagulation is as follows:

Prothrombin time	15 s (Control 16 s)
Partial thromboplastin time	82 s (Control 35 s)
Thrombin time	9 s (Control 9 s)
Platelet count	$212 \times 10^9/l$
Factor VIII assay	< 2 IU/l

a) What has happened?

....

2.7

A 22 year old male nurse presents with a three day history of nausea and vomiting. His admission biochemistry is shown below.

Na	135 mmol/l
Albumin	40 g/l
Alkaline phosphatase	110 IU/l
Gamma GT	28 IU/l
AST	40 IU/l
ALT	35 IU/l
Bilirubin	27 μmol/l

Over the next 24 hrs he continues to vomit and develops diarrhoea. His subsequent investigations are shown:

Na	132 mmol/l
Albumin	40 g/l
Alkaline phosphatase	115 IU/l
Gamma GT	36 IU/l
AST	45 IU/l
ALT	36 IU/l
Bilirubin	60 umol/l

a) What is the likely underlying diagnosis?

....

b) What tests are available to make this diagnosis?

....

....

2.8

A 38 year old lady, with a deforming arthropathy, develops dyspnoea. The following are her arterial blood gases:

pH   7.45

PaO_2 8.2 kPa

$PaCO_2$ 3.0 kPa

a) Suggest a possible diagnosis?

....

b) What is likely to happen to the above results when she undergoes exercise?

....

2.9

A plethoric 48 year old man is noted to have an Hb of 17 g/dl and a PCV of 0.56. Blood volume studies show the following:

	$^{125}I\,HSA$	^{51}Cr	*Predicted*
Plasma volume (l)	2.3	2.4	3.0
Red cell volume (l)	2.1	2.2	2.3
Blood volume (l)	4.4	4.6	5.3

a) What is the diagnosis?

....

2.10

A 30 year old lady gives a 2 year history of infertility following cessation of the oral contraceptive pill. The following is the result of anterior pituitary function testing:

Time	Glucose	Cortisol	GH	PL	FSH	LH	TSH	E2
	mmol/l	nmol/l	mu/l	mu/l	u/l	u/l	mu/l	pmol/l
0	4.2	600	0.5	950	3	10	< 1.0	< 100
30	1.4	900	1.0	990	11	> 50	7.0	
60	2.0	950	30	980	11	> 50	5.5	
90	2.6	970	15					
120	3.4	800	10					

a) What is the biochemical diagnosis?

....

b) What other symptoms may she have noticed?

....

....

DATA INTERPRETATION PAPER 3

1. Time available: 45 minutes.

2. Answer **all 10 of the following questions** in the spaces provided.

3. When asked (for example) to list 3 diagnoses or investigations, one line will be provided for each answer. If more than the required number of answers are given, the additional answers will not be scored.

4. Go over your answers until the 45 minutes are up. You can then check your answers against the correct answers and teaching notes for this paper as given on page 141 onwards.

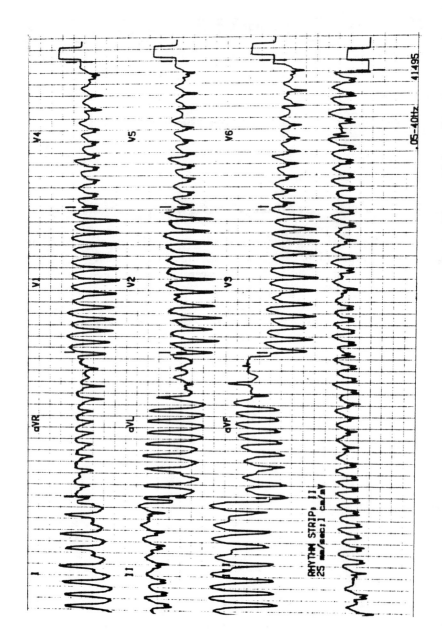

Figure 5

3.1

The ECG shown opposite (Fig. 5) is from a 58 year old who presented with an episode of epigastric pain.

a) What electrocardiographic diagnosis can be made from this ECG?

....

Paper 3

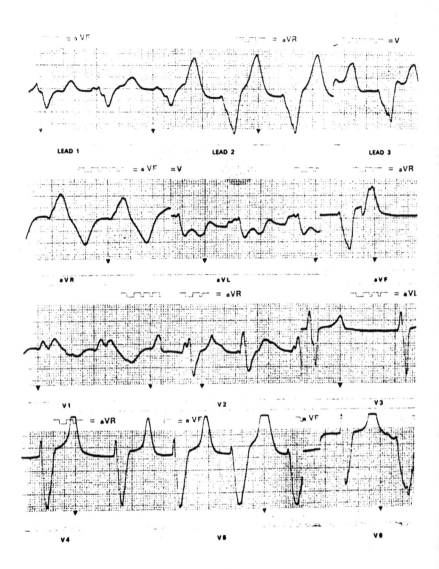

Figure 6

3.2

A 78 year old was admitted to casualty following a seizure. Her admission electrocardiograph is shown opposite.

a) What is the likely cause of the ECG findings?

....

Paper 3

3.3

A 35 year old female presents to medical outpatients with a two year history of dyspnoea.

She subsequently attended the Lung Laboratory for pulmonary function tests.

PaO_2	10 kPa
$PaCO_2$	3.9 kPA
FEV_1	1.8 l
FVC	2.0 l
TLC	2.3 l

a) What pulmonary function abnormality is shown?

....

b) What is the residual volume result likely to show?

....

c) What are the likely diagnostic possibilities in this case?

....

....

....

d) What further investigations are indicated?

....

....

....

3.4

An 18 year old woman attends the outpatient clinic complaining of tiredness and breathlessness. Systematic enquiry, past medical history and investigations for blood loss are unremarkable.

Hb	8.9 g/dl
MCV	74 fl
MCH	22.2 pg
MCHC	29.9 g/dl
WBC	6.4×10^9/l
Platelets	412×10^9/l
Ferritin	4 ng/l

After treatment with ferrous sulphate 200 mg, three times a day, for three months her repeat full blood count is as follows:

Hb	9.0 g/dl
MCV	73 fl
MCH	23.1 pg
MCHC	29.1 g/dl
WBC	5.8×10^9/l
Platelets	394×10^9/l
Ferritin	6 ng/l

a) Give three causes that may have contributed to her initial anaemia?

....

....

....

b) What is the most likely cause for the results at three months?

....

3.5

A 78 year old female was found, unconscious, behind her front door by a neighbour.

Below are the results of admission investigations.

Na	156	mmol/l
K	5.0	mmol/l
Cl	121	mmol/l
Bic	19	mmol/l
Urea	13.2	mmol/l
Creatinine	170	umol/l

Urinalysis	Haem	+ + +
	Gluc	+ + +
	Ketone bodies	-

a) What are the diagnoses?

....

....

....

....

b) What further investigations should be carried out?

....

....

....

3.6

A 42 year old man is admitted with jaundice and breathlessness. He is noted to have gynaecomastia.

Hb	7.2 g/dl	Bilirubin	64 μmol/l
Retics	7%	AST	98 IU/l
Platelets	137 x 10^9/l	ALT	104 IU/l
WBC	4.2 x 10^9/l	LDH	680 IU/l
Film	Target cells	GammaGT	284 IU/l
	Microspherocytes	Cholesterol	12.7 mmol/l
	Polychromasia	Triglycerides	18.3 mmol/l

a) What is the likely diagnosis?

....

3.7

A 57 year old woman, previously on treatment for Stage IIB Hodgkin's disease, presents with malaise, weight loss and bruising.

Hb	8.3 g/dl
MCV	87 fl
WBC	93.4 x 10^9/l
Neut	4.3 x 10^9/l
Lymph	3.8 x 10^9/l
Myeloblasts	84.3 x 10^9/l
Platelets	68 x 10^9/l

a) What diagnosis can be made from the above figures?

....

b) How is this related to the past medical history?

....

....

3.8

The following are the results from a 15 year old girl who was referred by her General Practitioner:

LH   > 40 U/l
Oestradiol   90 pmol/l

a) What diagnosis is likely?

....

b) What further investigations are required?

....

....

c) What treatment is indicated?

....

d) What is the probability of the condition affecting any future children of the patient?

....

3.9

The diagram below shows the plasma lipid fractionation from a fasting control and patient A.

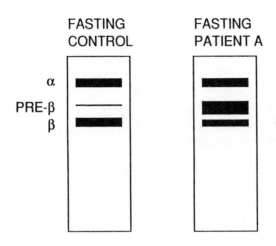

a) What is the diagnosis of patient A?

....

b) What clinical signs may be found in this patient?

....

....

Paper 3

3.10

The following is an ABO grouping from a 22 year old potential blood donor:

Serum grouping

A_1 cells   +
A_2 cells   -
B   cells   +
O   cells   -

Red cell grouping

	Patient cells	A_1	A_2	Controls B	OCells
AntiB	-	-	-	+	-
AntiA	+	+	+	-	-
AntiA$_1$B	+	+	+	+	-
PUP	-				

		A_1	A_2	B	OCells
AntiA$_1$	-	+	-	-	-

(+ = Agglutination)
(- = No agglutination)

a) What is the patient's blood group?

....

b) What other feature is present?

....

54

DATA INTERPRETATION PAPER 4

1. Time available: 45 minutes.

2. Answer **all 10 of the following questions** in the spaces provided.

3. When asked (for example) to list 3 diagnoses or investigations, one line
    will be provided for each answer. If more than the required number of
    answers are given, the additional answers will not be scored.

4. Go over your answers until the 45 minutes are up. You can then check
    your answers against the correct answers and teaching notes for this
    paper as given on page 145 onwards.

Paper 4

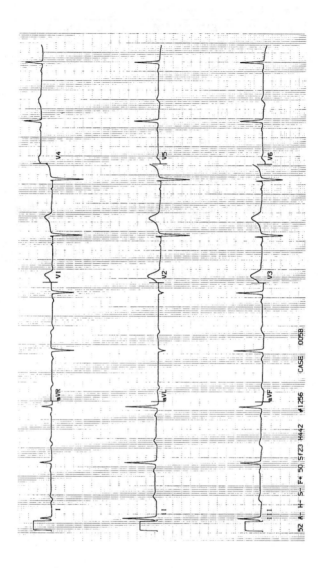

Figure 7

4.1

a) What abnormality is shown on the ECG shown opposite (Fig. 7)?

   ....

b) What underlying conditions predispose to this abnormality?

   ....

   ....

   ....

   ....

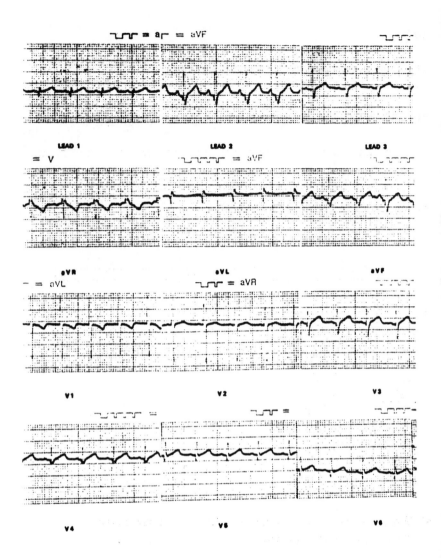

Figure 8

Paper 4

4.2

The ECG shown opposite (Fig. 8) was taken from a 22 year old male admitted for elective placement of a feeding gastrostomy.

a) What two abnormalities are seen?

....

....

b) Suggest two possible causes.

....

....

4.3

A 31 year old, with chronic lethargy, presents with back pain.

Hb	9 g/dl
MCV	89 fl
Ca^{++}	2.05 mmol/l
Phosphate	1.65 mmol/l
Albumin	39 g/l
Urate	0.6 mmol/l
pO_2	11.5 kPa
pCO_2	2.5 kPa

a) What investigations would help determine the nature of the calcium/phosphate balance?

....

....

b) What is the unifying diagnosis for the above results?

....

Paper 4

4.4

This is the cardiac catheter result from a patient admitted for assessment for cardiac surgery. Clinical examination is unremarkable.

	Pressure mmHg	O₂ Saturation %
R. atrium	10	80
R. ventricle	33/0	-
Pulm. artery	33/12	-
L. atrium	12	-
L. ventricle	102/0	-
Aorta	120/66	-
Femoral vein	-	62
Femoral artery	-	94

a) What cardiac diagnosis can be made from these figures?

....

b) What are the typical ECG findings of this condition?

....

....

4.5

A 68 year old woman presents with bruising, dysuria and pyrexia.

Hb	10.0 g/dl	
Retics	7%	
Platelets	$34 \times 10^9/l$	
WBC	$15.3 \times 10^9/l$	
Prothrombin time		23 s (Control 15 s)
Partial thromboplastin time		61 s (Control 35 s)
Thrombin time		14 s (Control 9 s)
Fibrinogen	1 g/l	(N.R. 2-4 g/l)

Urine: Pus + + +
                  RBC + + +

a) What is the haematological diagnosis?

....

b) What two further tests would you do to confirm this?

....

....

4.6

A 62 year old man is referred to a haematology clinic for investigation of lassitude.

Hb	10.1 g/dl
MCV	90 fl
ESR	100 mm in 1st hr
Na	118 mmol/l
K	3.8 mmol/l
Cl	86 mmol/l
Urea	12.6 mmol/l
Creatinine	260 μmol/l

a) What two further investigations would be useful in making the diagnosis?

....

....

b) What two diagnoses are likely?

....

....

4.7

A 34 year old man, with a history of asthma since childhood presents with a six month history of worsening dyspnoea and cough productive of green-brown sputum.

Hb	14.3 g/dl
WBC	$7.3 \times 10^9/l$
Neut	$4.2 \times 10^9/l$
Lymph	$1.5 \times 10^9/l$
Eosinophils	$1.1 \times 10^9/l$
Monocytes	$0.4 \times 10^9/l$
Basophils	$0.1 \times 10^9/l$
Platelets	$327 \times 10^9/l$
PaO_2	11.7 kPa
$PaCO_2$	5.0 kPa
pH	7.42
CXR	Patchy shadowing right upper zone

a) What is the likely diagnosis?

....

b) What two further investigations would be useful in making the diagnosis?

....

....

4.8

A 47 year old presents with general malaise and occipital headache. The following is the result of CSF examination:

Pressure	17 cm H_2O
Cells	$0.12 \times 10^9/l$
Lymphocytes	55 %
Protein	1.4 g/l
Cytology	No malignant cells seen

a) What diagnosis is likely from the above results?

....

b) What further investigations would assist in making the diagnosis?

....

....

....

....

4.9

Below are the results of a glucose tolerance test of a 25 year old female who was given a 50g glucose load.

Time (Mins)	Glucose(mmol/l)	Urine Glucose	Ketones
0	4.7	0	0
30	6.5		
60	7.8	+	0
90	6.7		
120	4.4	+ +	0

a) What diagnosis is suggested by the above figures?

....

b) With what conditions is it associated?

....

....

4.10

The osmotic fragility curve shown below was obtained from a 13 year old boy
with a haemoglobin of 9 g/dl and a negative Coomb's test.

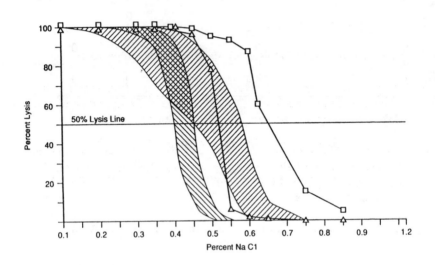

REPORT:- RED CELL OSMOTIC FRAGILITY

Normal range at 0 hrs., and pH 7.4

Normal range after incubation at 37°C for 24 hrs.

△——△ Patient at 20°C

□——□ Patient after 24 hrs. at 37°C

M.C.F. = 0.52%   (Normal 0.40 - 0.445%)

= 0.67%   after 24 hrs. at 37°C
(Normal 0.465 - 0.590%)

a) What diagnosis is suggested?

....

DATA INTERPRETATION PAPER 5

1. Time available: 45 minutes.

2. Answer **all 10 of the following questions** in the spaces provided.

3. When asked (for example) to list 3 diagnoses or investigations, one line will be provided for each answer. If more than the required number of answers are given, the additional answers will not be scored.

4. Go over your answers until the 45 minutes are up. You can then check your answers against the correct answers and teaching notes for this paper as given on page 150 onwards.

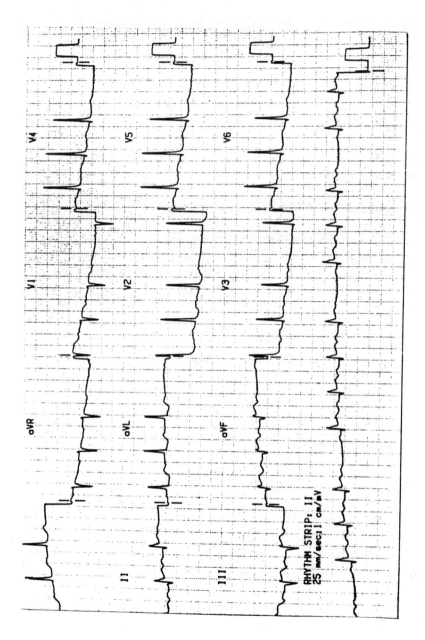

Figure 9

5.1

The ECG opposite (Fig. 9) is of an 82 year old male, on digoxin, admitted to Coronary Care.

a) What rhythm disturbance is shown?

....

b) What is the likely underlying cause?

....

5.2

A 32 year old man presents with tiredness two years after exploratory craniotomy.

Hb	7.2 g/dl
WBC	$4.3 \times 10^9/l$
Platelets	$122 \times 10^9/l$
MCV	120 fl
MCH	37 pg
Film	macrocytosis
Reticulocytes	1%

a) What 2 further investigations are indicated?

....

....

b) What is the likely cause of the anaemia?

....

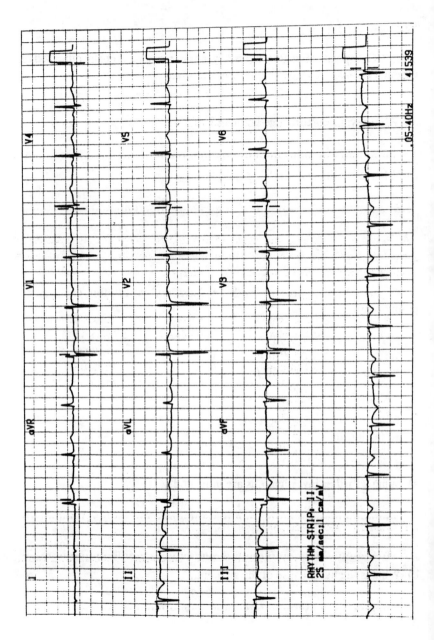

Figure 10

5.3

The ECG shown oposite (Fig. 10) was taken from a 29 year old pregnant female who presented with pleuritic chest pain.

a) What abnormality is shown on this ECG?

....

5.4

A 78 year old lady is admitted to a geriatric ward for assessment of breathlessness. On examination there is a small right-sided pleural effusion. Below are the results of routine blood analysis.

Na	130 mmol/l	Hb	10.8 g/dl
K	3.5 mmol/l	WBC	7.9 x 10^9/l
Cl	103 mmol/l	Platelets	180 x 10^9/l
Bic	22 mmol/l	film	anisocytosis
Urea	5.1 mmol/l		with mild
Creatinine	95 μmol/l		macrocytosis
AST	38 IU/l		
ALT	40 IU/l		
LDH	220 IU/l		
CK	225 IU/l		
Gamma GT	38 IU/l		
Alk Phosp	115 IU/l		

a) Suggest a likely underlying diagnosis.

....

5.5

The following are the biochemistry results from an 79 year old woman admitted to hospital with back pain and depression:

Na	132 mmol/l	Ca^{++}	2.93 mmol/l
K	4.2 mmol/l	Phosp	1.20 mmol
Cl	108 mmol/l	Albumin	26 g/l
Bic	23 mmol/l	Bilirubin	7 μmol/l
Urea	11.3 mmol/l	Alk Phosp	107 UI/l
Creatinine	100 umol/l	AST	17 IU/l
Total protein	103 g/l	ALT	14 IU/l
		LDH	247 IU/l
		GammaGT	13 IU/l

Urine: Protein   + + +
               Blood   -

a) What is the likely underlying diagnosis?

....

b) What further investigations would be useful in confirming the diagnosis?

....

....

....

....

5.6

An otherwise fit 68 year old woman was investigated for recent onset of deafness. Systematic enquiry, aside from diffuse 'aches and pains', is unremarkable.

Albumin	38 g/l	LDH	220 IU/l
Total protein	70 g/l	Alk Phosp	280 IU/l
AST	20 IU/l	GammaGT	28 IU/l
ALT	39 IU/l	Bilirubin	14 IU/l

ESR   21 mm 1st hr

Rhinne Test	Left	Right
Air Conduction	+	+ +
Bone Conduction	+/-	+

Weber Test		
	+	+ +

(+ represents intensity)

a) What three further investigations would be useful?

....

....

....

b) What are the most likely diagnoses from the above results?

....

....

c) What are the implications for treatment of the underlying condition?

....

5.7

A thirty four year old is admitted with a haematemesis.

pH   7.30
pCO_2 2.9 kPa
Bic   15 mmol/l
pO_2 11.4 kPa

RBC Transketolase activity > 60% Activity

a) What two biochemical diagnoses can be implied from the above results?

....

....

5.8

The following are the full blood count results recorded during the admission of a 14 year old boy who presented with cellulitis and buccal ulceration:

		Day 1	*Day 10*	*Day 20*
Hb	(g/dl)	13.2	12.9	13.0
WBC	$(x\ 10^9/l)$	3.4	6.8	3.0
Neut	$(x\ 10^9/l)$	0.7	4.3	0.6
Lymph	$(x\ 10^9/l)$	2.7	2.5	2.4
Plat	$(x\ 10^9/l)$	328	310	316

a) What is the diagnosis?

....

5.9

A 52 year old man becomes unwell whilst at work in a cigarette factory. He gives a three day history of watery motions and appears restless and agitated on admission.

Na	131 mmol/l	Hb	12.2 g/dl
K	3.5 mmol/l	WBC	$11 \times 10^9/l$
Cl	90 mmol/l	Platelets	$221 \times 10^9/l$
Bic	15 mmol/l		
Urea	11.1 mmol/l	Temp	38°C
Creatinine	122 μmol/l		
pO2	7.0 kPa	Urinalysis:	
			blood + +
			protein -

a) What further investigations are required?

....

....

....

b) What is the differential diagnosis?

....

....

5.10

The figure below shows the results of pulmonary function tests of a 52 year old female post-bronchodilator therapy.

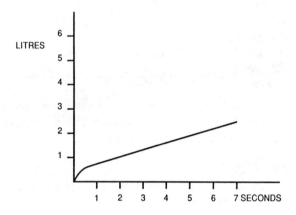

a) What abnormality is shown?

....

DATA INTERPRETATION PAPER 6

1. Time available: 45 minutes.

2. Answer **all 10 of the following questions** in the spaces provided.

3. When asked (for example) to list 3 diagnoses or investigations, one line will be provided for each answer. If more than the required number of answers are given, the additional answers will not be scored.

4. Go over your answers until the 45 minutes are up. You can then check your answers against the correct answers and teaching notes for this paper as given on page 155 onwards.

Paper 6

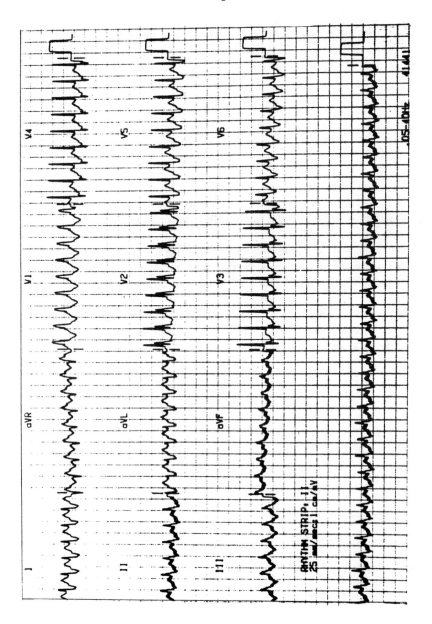

Figure 11

6.1

The ECG shown opposite (Fig. 11) is of a 48 year old male admitted to Coronary Care following an episode of collapse. Clinically he is shocked.

a) What rhythm disturbances are shown?

....

....

b) What treatment is indicated?

....

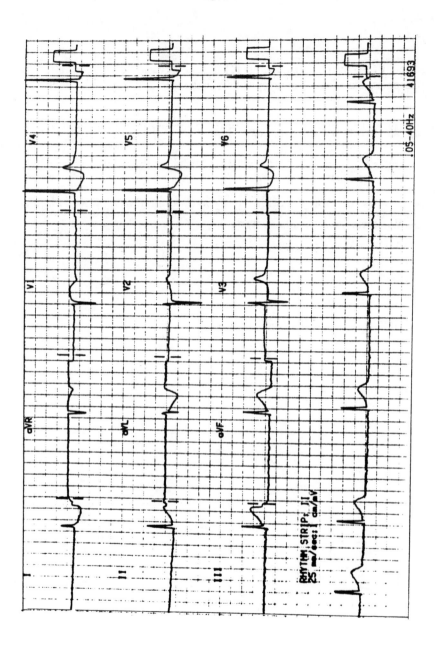

Figure 12

6.2

a) What two diagnoses can be made from the ECG shown opposite (Fig. 12)?

....

....

6.3

An 18 year old male presented with bruising.

FBC:

Hb	8.2 g/dl
WBC	$1.3 \times 10^9/l$
Platelets	$18 \times 10^9/l$

Marrow cytochemistry:

Sudan Black	+
Myeloperoxidase	+
Periodic Acid Schiff	-
Non-specific Esterase	-

a) What is the diagnosis?

....

6.4

The diagram shown is a pedigree from a family with a genetic condition.

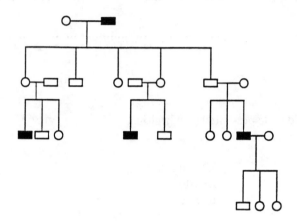

■ = AFFECTED MALE
□ = NORMAL MALE
● = AFFECTED FEMALE
○ = NORMAL FEMALE

a) What is the mode of inheritance?

....

b) Name two conditions that show this mode of inheritance.

....

....

6.5

A thirty eight year old woman is noted to have glycosuria. Below are some of the further investigations which were carried out.

Anterior pituitary function (IV insulin 0.3 U/kg)

Time	Glucose mmol/l	Cortisol nmol/l
0	6.1	290
30	2.6	300
60	2.7	510
90	3.5	480
120	5.0	470

a) What abnormality is shown?

....

b) What other tests should be carried out?

....

c) Give a cause for this abnormality?

....

6.6

A 28 year old black woman attends her GP for an insurance medical. The following is the result of her blood analysis:

Hb	13.8 g/dl
WBC	$8.7 \times 10^9/l$
Platelets	$190 \times 10^9/l$
MCV	78 fl
MCH	27.5 pg
MCHC	35 g/dl
Retics	7%
Sickle	+ve

Hb Electrophoresis:

HbA	0%
HbA_2	4.4%
HbS	70%
HbF	25%

a) What further investigations are required?

....

....

b) Give two possible diagnoses.

....

....

6.7

A thirty-five year old female presents to the dermatology department for investigation of a skin rash.

AST   42 IU/l
ALT   40 IU/l
LDH   220 IU/l
GammaGT   42 IU/l
Alk Phosp   125 IU/l

Hb   11.1 g/dl
WBC $6.8 \times 10^9/l$
Platelets $234 \times 10^9/l$
Ferritin   364 pg/l

Urine:
        PBG   -
        ALA   -
        Porphyrins   +

Faecal porphrins   -   (PBG = Porphobilinogen)
                       (ALA = 5-Aminolaevulinate)

a) What is the likely diagnosis?

    ....

b) What treatment may be helpful?

    ....

6.8

A 54 year old, with a past history of surgery and radiotherapy for abdominal lymphoma, has the following results at follow up:

Na	130 mmol/l
K	3.0 mmol/l
Cl	110 mmol/l
Bic	10 mmol/l
Urea	6.0 mmol/l
Creatinine	118 μmol/l
pO$_2$	11 kPa
pCO$_2$	2.9 kPa
pH	7.27

a) What biochemical abnormalities are shown?

....

....

....

b) Suggest a likely cause.

....

6.9

A 10 year old caucasian child is admitted with severe abdominal pain.

Hb	8.7 g/dl
WBC	$4.7 \times 10^9/l$
Platelets	$314 \times 10^9/l$
MCV	80 fl
MCH	24 pg
Film	Mild hypochromia
	Punctate basophilia noted

a) What is the likely diagnosis?

....

b) How would you confirm the diagnosis?

....

....

6.10

A 33 year old female is admitted from Casualty. She gives a history of recent vomiting and diarrhoea.

Na	135 mmol/l
K	3.1 mmol/l
Cl	98 mmol/l
Bicarbonate	18 mmol/l
Urea	3.2 mmol/l
Creatinine	180 μmol/l
Glucose	2.1 mmol/l
Serum osmolality	320 mmol/kg

a) What biochemical abnormalities are present?

....

....

....

....

b) What is the likely cause?

....

DATA INTERPRETATION PAPER 7

1. Time available: 45 minutes.

2. Answer **all 10 of the following questions** in the spaces provided.

3. When asked (for example) to list 3 diagnoses or investigations, one line will be provided for each answer. If more than the required number of answers are given, the additional answers will not be scored.

4. Go over your answers until the 45 minutes are up. You can then check your answers against the correct answers and teaching notes for this paper as given on page 161 onwards.

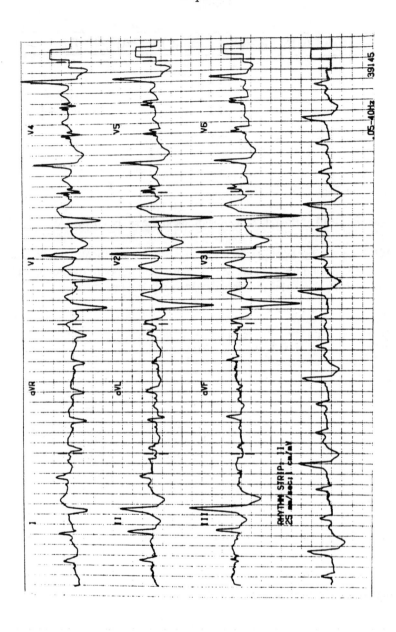

Figure 13

7.1

a) What abnormalities are seen in the ECG shown opposite (Fig. 13)?

....

....

7.2

A 58 year old man is seen for investigation of polyuria. He is noted to have one finger-breadth hepatomegaly.

Na	135 mmol/l	Fe	51 μmol/l
K	3.1 mmol/l	TIBC	52 μmol/l
Cl	98 mmol/l	% Saturation	100%
Bic	18 mmol/l		
Urea	3.2 mmol/l	AST	38 IU/l
Creatinine	180 μmol/l	ALT	66 IU/l
Glucose	15.8 mmol/l	Alk Phosp	90 IU/l
		Gamma GT	46 IU/l
		LDH	230 IU/l
		Bilirubin	17 μmol/l
		Albumin	44 g/l
		Globulins	28 g/l

a) What two further investigations would be of benefit?

....

....

b) Suggest two likely diagnoses.

....

....

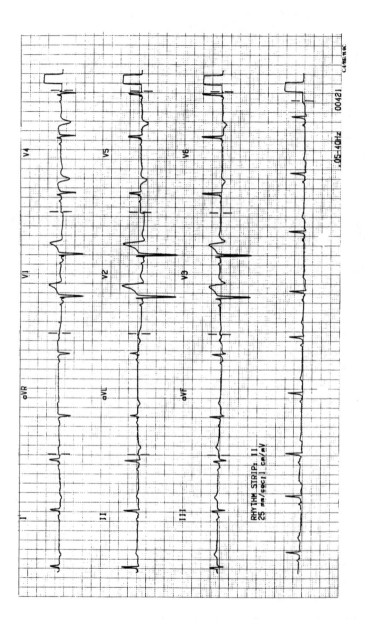

Figure 14

7.3

A 46 year old man presents with a left hemiparesis six months after a myocardial infarction.

His current ECG is shown opposite (Fig. 14).

a) Give two possible diagnoses.

....

....

7.4

A male child born at 32 weeks gestation develops bruising two days after delivery. A coagulation specimen taken from the umbilical vein catheter gives the following results:

	Patient	Control
Prothrombin time	38 s	15 s
Partial thromboplastin time	160 s	37 s
Thrombin time	28 s	7 s
Platelets	$137 \times 10^9/l$	

a) What is the likely cause of these figures?

....

7.5

The following are results of investigations of an 82 year old female who was found unconscious by her neighbour:

Hb	14 g/dl
WBC	7.2×10^9/l
Platelets	430×10^9/l
MCV	77 fl
HCT	0.53
Ca^{++}	2.73 mmol/l
Phosphate	1.38 mmol/l
Alk Phosp	250 IU/l
GammaGT	30 IU/l
Globulins	31 g/l
Protein	88 g/l

a) What further investigations are required?

....

....

....

....

b) What is the likely diagnosis?

....

7.6

A 42 year old is admitted to a medical ward with acute onset of atrial fibrillation.

The following are the results of biochemical investigations:

Urea	8.0 mmol/l
Creatinine	110 μmol/l
Total Protein	68 g/l
Globulin	22 g/l
Cholesterol	10.4 mmol/l
Total T4	27 nmol/l
TSH	2.5 mU/l
T3	1.4 nmol/l
Free T4	15 pmol/l
AST	32 IU/l
ALT	38 IU/l
Alk Phosp	110 IU/l
Gamma GT	20 IU/l

a) What further investigations are required?

....

....

b) What diagnoses are indicated from the above data?

....

....

7.7

A 32 year old man continues to suffer dyspepsia after surgery for peptic ulceration. His symptoms have not been controlled by H_2 receptor or proton pump, inhibitors.

The following is the result of insulin hypoglycaemia testing after all medication was withdrawn:

Time	Glucose (mmol/l)	pH	Conc. (mEq/l)
0	4.6	1.8	33
(IV Soluble insulin 16 IU)			
30	2.0	1.6	54
60	1.9	1.3	84
90	3.2	1.2	94
120	4.8	1.2	88

a) What does the above test reveal?

....

7.8

A 47 year old man is noted to have splenomegaly.

Hb	8.1 g/dl
MCV	92 fl
WBC	4.3×10^9/l
Neut	1.0×10^9/l
Mono	0.1×10^9/l
Lymphoid	3.2×10^9/l
Platelets	67×10^9/l
Tartrate resistant acid phosphatase	+ve reaction

a) What is the diagnosis?

....

7.9

What diagnosis can be made from these cardiac catheter results of a 45 year old woman.

	Pressures (mmHg)	Normal range (mmHg)
Right atrium	5	0-8
Right ventricle	30/7	15-30/0-8
Pulmonary artery	30/16	15-30/6-16
Left ventricle	190/6	90-140/4-12
Cardiac output	3.8l/min/m^2	2.8-4.2l/min/m^2
BP	145/72	

a) What abnormality is shown?

....

b) What corrective surgery is indicated?

....

7.10

A 48 year old female with long standing dyspnoea presents with a right pleural effusion.

Below is the result of pleural aspirate:

Protein	36 g/l
Glucose	2.2 mmol/l
Amylase	180 IU/l
Rheumatoid factor	1/320
Complement	
CH_{50}	undetectable
C_4	> 4.5 mg/l

a) What other investigations are required?

....

....

b) What is the likely cause of the effusion?

....

DATA INTERPRETATION PAPER 8

1. Time available: 45 minutes.

2. Answer **all 10 of the following questions** in the spaces provided.

3. When asked (for example) to list 3 diagnoses or investigations, one line will be provided for each answer. If more than the required number of answers are given, the additional answers will not be scored.

4. Go over your answers until the 45 minutes are up. You can then check your answers against the correct answers and teaching notes for this paper as given on page 165 onwards.

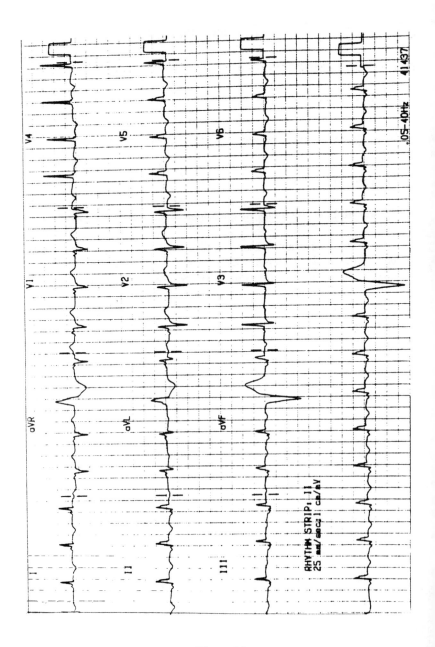

Figure 15

8.1

a) What abnormalities are seen on the ECG shown opposite (Fig. 15)?

....

....

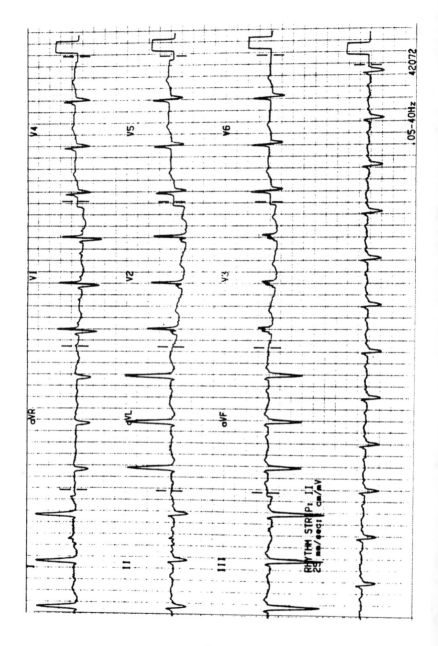

Figure 16

8.2

a) What abnormalities are shown on the ECG shown opposite (Fig. 16)?

....

b) What treatment is indicated?

....

8.3

A 42 year old man with inflammatory bowel disease is noted to be pale.

Hb	8.7 g/dl
WBC	$10.2 \times 10^9/l$
MCV	104 fl
Platelets	$550 \times 10^9/l$
Film	Polychromasia
	Fragmented RBC
	Spherocytes
Urine	Haemosiderin + +

a) What is the haematological diagnosis?

....

b) What is the likely aetiology?

....

8.4

A 72 year old man was admitted to hospital after an episode of chest pain. His initial investigations were as follows:

Na	136 mmol/l	Hb	12.2 g/dl
K	4.9 mmol/l	WBC	14×10^9/l
Cl	99 mmol/l	Platelets	282×10^9/l
Bic	17 mmol/l	HbA$_1$c	4.0%
Urea	12.2 mmol/l		
Creatinine	132 μmol/l	Urinalysis	Haem -
			Glucose + + +
			Protein trace
			Ketones + +

a) Which two immediate investigations are indicated?

....

....

b) What is the differential diagnosis?

....

....

....

8.5

A 57 year old woman presents with weight loss. She has the following results:

Hb	18.7 g/dl
WBC	6.29 x 10^9/l
Platelets	175 x 10^9/l
MCV	93.9 fl
MCH	32.9 pg
HCT	0.56
Na	136 mmol/l
Urea	5.5 mmol/l
Creatinine	82 μmol/l
PaO$_2$	10.5 kPa

Bone marrow examination: normal
Blood volume studies: elevated red cell mass

a) What two further investigations would be useful?

....

....

b) Give four possible causes for these findings.

....

....

....

....

8.6

The following results were obtained from a 25 year old male, who was admitted as an emergency, with vomiting:

Na	152 mmol/l
K	3.2 mmol/l
Bic	8 mmol/l
Urea	14.2 mmol/l
Creatinine	110 μmol/l
Hb	17 g/dl
WBC	16.6 x 10^9/l
Prothrombin time	21 s Control 14 s
Urine	Reducing sugar +ve

a) What further investigations are required?

....

....

....

b) What is the differential diagnosis?

....

....

....

8.7

A 65 year old man has the following blood count:

Hb	8.2 g/dl
Platelets	386 x 10^9/l
WBC	26.2 x 10^9/l
Neut	17.2 x 10^9/l
Lymph	3.39 x 10^9/l
Myelocytes	4.51 x 10^9/l
Metamyelocytes	0.52 x 10^9/l
Blasts	0.58 x 10^9/l
Film	Nucleated RBC 2%
Marrow aspirate	Dry tap

a) What three investigations are indicated?

....

....

....

b) Name two possible diagnoses.

....

....

8.8

The protein electrophoresis shown is taken from a patient admitted as an emergency to the Intensive Therapy Unit.

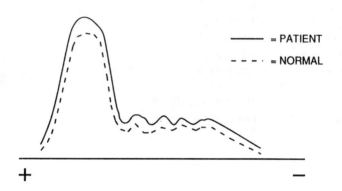

——— = PATIENT

- - - · = NORMAL

+   −

a) What abnormality is shown?

....

b) Suggest two possible causes.

....

....

8.9

A 22 year old male presents to his GP with tiredness and lymphadenopathy.

Hb	10.3 g/dl
WBC	$7.8 \times 10^9/l$
Platelets	$134 \times 10^9/l$
Monospot Test	Positive
Anti Epstein-Barr	IgM Negative
Virus antibody	IgG Negative

a) What further investigation should be carried out?

....

b) What is the likely diagnosis?

....

8.10

Below is the biochemistry of a 32 year old male noted to have glycosuria.

Na	135 mmol/l
K	4.0 mmol/l
Cl	104 mmol/l
Bic	25 mmol/l
Urea	4.0 mmol/l
Plasma creatinine	60 μmol/l
Urine creatinine	7.8 mmol/l
Urine vol (24 hrs)	1440 ml

a) What abnormality of renal function is shown?

....

b) What is the likely cause of this abnormality?

....

1. Time available: 45 minutes.

2. Answer **all 10 of the following questions** in the spaces provided.

3. When asked (for example) to list 3 diagnoses or investigations, one line will be provided for each answer. If more than the required number of answers are given, the additional answers will not be scored.

4. Go over your answers until the 45 minutes are up. You can then check your answers against the correct answers and teaching notes for this paper as given on page 170 onwards.

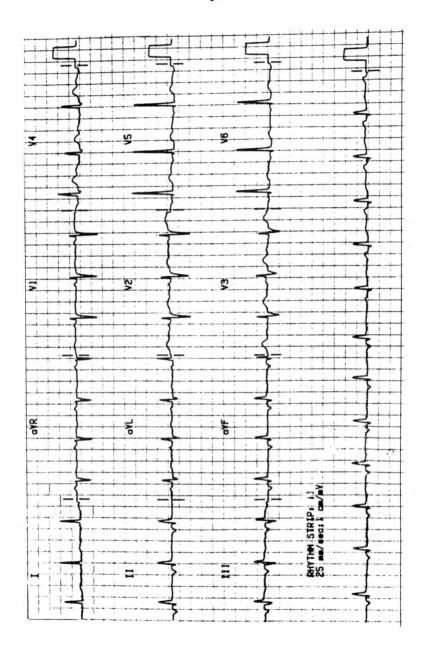

Figure 17

9.1

a) What abnormalities are seen in the ECG shown opposite (Fig. 17)?

....

....

9.2

The results below are from a 42 year old man with chronic liver disease.

	Patient	NR
Serum caeruloplasmin	450 mg/l	200-400 mg/l
Urinary copper	90 μg/day	< 50 μg/dy

a) What are the likely differential diagnoses?

....

....

b) What further investigations would be useful?

....

....

....

Paper 9

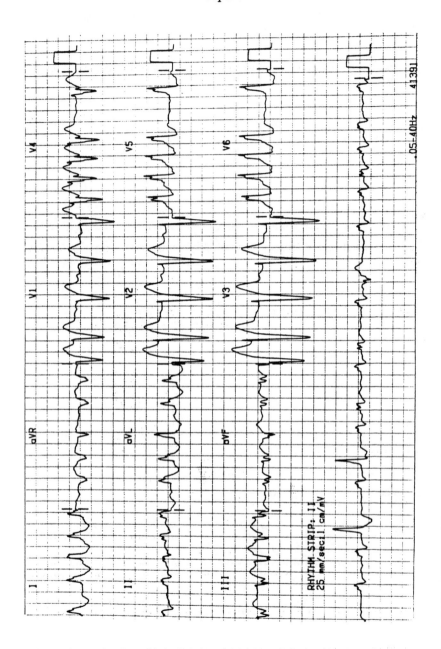

Figure 18

9.3

The ECG shown opposite (Fig. 18) is from a patient who was seen routinely at a medical clinic.

a) What is the main abnormality?

....

9.4

The results shown are from a 48 year old female under investigation for obesity.

Day	Dexamethasone (mg/day)	Urinary Free Cortisol (μmol/mol creatinine)
1	0	110
2	0	98
3	2	52
4	2	49
5	8	26
6	8	24

a) What is the diagnosis?

....

....

....

....

9.5

A 52 year old smoker attends for pulmonary function testing. The flow volume loop shown below is taken from this patient.

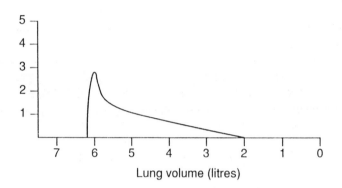

a) What is the diagnosis?

....

Expected Values:

Residual volume	0.5 litres
Total lung capacity	4.0 litres
Peak expiratory flow rate	6.0 litres/sec

9.6

Below is the result of ABO grouping.

	Patient serum
A$_1$ cells	0
A$_2$ cells	0
B cells	0
O cells	0

	Patient cells	Controls A1	A2	B	O	Cells
AntiB	0	0	0	+ +	0	
AntiA	0	+ +	+ +	0	0	
AntiAB	0	+ +	+ +	+ +	0	
PUP	0					

(+ = Agglutination)
(0 = No Agglutination)

a) What is the blood group?

....

b) What is the unusual feature of this grouping?

....

9.7

A 48 year old man presents with weight loss, joint pains, loose bowel motions
and fatigue. Below are the results of routine haematology.

Hb	8.4 g/dl
WBC	4.7 x 10^9/l
MCV	108 fl
Platelets	342 x 10^9/l
Film	Macrocytes and microcytes seen
	Target cells and Howell-Jolly bodies + + +
	Irregularly contracted RBC seen

a) What two haematological diagnoses are evident?

....

....

b) What is the likely underlying diagnosis?

....

9.8

A 22 year old female, on no medication, presents with a left calf deep venous
thrombosis.

	Patient	Control
Prothrombin time	14 s	13 s
Partial thromboplastin time	59 s	37 s
Thrombin time	9 s	9 s
Platelets	364 x 10^9/l	

a) What is the diagnosis?

....

9.9

A 4 year old male child is admitted with malaise, fever and diarrhoea.

Hb	9.2 g/dl
WBC	$8.4 \times 10^9/l$
Platelets	$37 \times 10^9/l$
Urea	26 mmol/l
Creatinine	$240 \, \mu mol/l$
Bilirubin	27 umol/l

a) What three further investigations should be performed?

....

....

....

b) What is the likely diagnosis?

....

9.10

A 45 year old woman complains of urinary frequency. She undergoes a standard water deprivation test starting at 08.30 hrs

Time (hrs)	Plasma osmolality (mmol/kg)	Urine osmolality (mmol/kg)	Weight (kg)
0	290	110	60
3	300	122	58.2
6	312	122	56.4
8	325	130	55
(2 μg i.m. Desmopressin)			
10	-	320	-

a) What comments can be made on the above results?

....

....

....

b) Suggest a cause for these results.

....

DATA INTERPRETATION PAPER 10

1. Time available: 45 minutes.

2. Answer **all 10 of the following questions** in the spaces provided.

3. When asked (for example) to list 3 diagnoses or investigations, one line will be provided for each answer. If more than the required number of answers are given, the additional answers will not be scored.

4. Go over your answers until the 45 minutes are up. You can then check your answers against the correct answers and teaching notes for this paper as given on page 175 onwards.

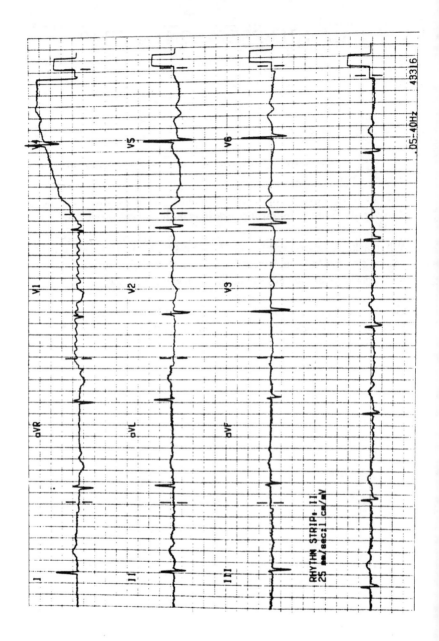

Figure 19

10.1

A 55 year old female is admitted with breathlessness. The ECG shown opposite (Fig. 19) was recorded on admission.

a) What abnormalities are shown?

....

....

....

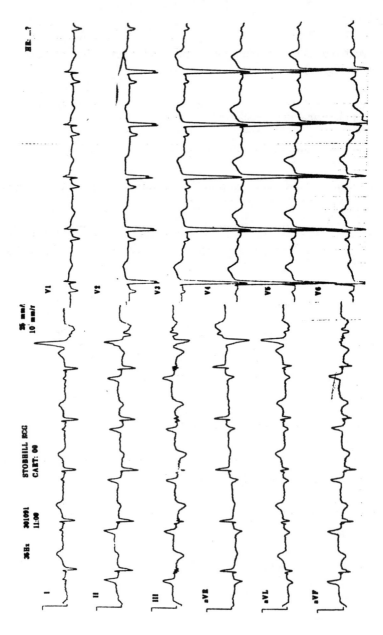

Figure 20

10.2

a) What is the likely cause for dyspnoea in this 68 year old woman?
See (Fig. 20) opposite.

....

10.3

A 25 year old school teacher is admitted to the dental hospital having bled
excessively after a tooth extraction.

The following results were obtained from samples collected simultaneously
in clotted and lithium heparin bottles. There was no evidence of haemolysis
in either sample:

Na	136 mmol/l	Na	135 mmol/l
K	6.9 mmol/l	K	3.9 mmol/l
Cl	101 mmol/l	Cl	100 mmol/l
Bic	28 mmol/l	Bic	27 mmol/l
Urea	5.2 mmol/l	Urea	5.2 mmol/l
Creatinine	69 μmol/l	Creatinine	69 μmol/l

a) What other investigation is required?

....

b) Suggest a possible underlying diagnosis.

....

Paper 10

10.4

A 22 year old female is admitted to hospital for investigation of a swollen left calf.

Below is the result of her admission coagulation screen.

	Patient	*Control*
Prothrombin time	17 s	16 s
Partial thromboplastin time	25 s	36 s
Thrombin time	10 s	9 s

a) What abnormality is shown?

    ....

b) Suggest three possible causes for this abnormality?

    ....

    ....

    ....

c) What action would you take to confirm this result?

    ....

10.5

A 35 year old female is noted to have diffuse lymphadenopathy and reactive lymphocytes in her blood film.

Below is the result of haematological investigations:

Hb	13.5 g/dl
WBC	$21 \times 10^9/l$
Platelets	$260 \times 10^9/l$
Monospot	positive

Cell marker studies on peripheral blood:

	Antigen	Percentage
Class II	HLA DR	78
Mature B	CD 22	2
T Cell Associated	CD 2	94
	CD 3	11
	CD 4	7
	CD 5	9
	CD 8	67
Other	CD 56	71

a) What three abnormalities are shown?

....

....

....

b) What is the likely diagnosis?

....

10.6

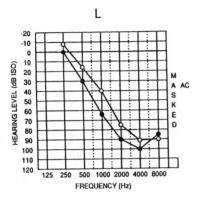

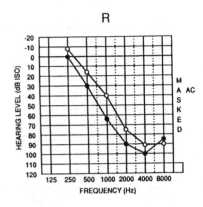

a) What abnormality can be seen in this audiogram of a 16 year old boy?

....

b) Suggest a possible aetiology.

....

10.7

A 37 year old woman presents with weight loss and irritability. She is noted to have an irregular, rapid heart rate.

The following results were obtained:

T_4	100 nmol/l
TSH	<0.1 mU/l
TBG	20 mg/ml
FreeT$_4$	20 pmol/l

a) What is the diagnosis?

....

10.8

A 31 year old with longstanding liver dysfunction is admitted with increasing abdominal distension.

Ascites is detected clinically and a therapeutic tap is performed.

Fluid amylase	174 U/l
Fluid glucose	6.9 mmol/l
Fluid lactate dehydrogenase	545 U/l
Fluid protein	33 g/l
WBC	400 cells/mm^3
Polymorphonuclear cells	50%

a) What other investigation is required?

....

b) What treatment is indicated?

....

10.9

A 78 year old man with carcinoma of the colon is admitted for surgery. The following are the results of his ABO blood grouping prior to surgery and immediately after surgery when blood transfusion was required:

Serum grouping

	Pre-op	*Post-op*
B Cells	+ +	+ +
A Cells	+ +	0

Cell grouping

Anti A	0	+ +
Anti B	0	0
Anti A,B	0	+ +
PUP	0	0

a) What blood groups are shown?

   ....

   ....

b) What has happened?

   ....

10.10

A 31 year old presents with abdominal pain and distension. Doppler ultrasound reveals a thrombosis of the portal vein.

Below are the results of investigations on admission.

Na	136 mmol/l	Hb	8.0 g/dl
K	4.2 mmol/l	WBC	3.2×10^9/l
Cl	101 mmol/l	Platelets	69×10^9/l
Bic	28 mmol/l		
Urea	5.2 mmol/l		
Creatinine	69 μmol/l		

AST	353 IU/l	
ALT	55 IU/l	
Alk Phosp	133 IU/l	Urinalysis:
Gamma GT	27 IU/l	
LDH	856 IU/l	colour red/brown
Albumin	27 g/l	RBC -ve
		protein trace

a) What three further investigations may be helpful in obtaining the diagnosis?

....

....

....

b) What is the underlying diagnosis?

....

1.1

a) Wolf-Parkinson-White syndrome Type B.
b) 24 hr tape examination.
   Exercise tolerance testing.

Wolf-Parkinson-White syndrome is due to the presence of an abnormal conduction pathway (the bundle of Kent) between the atrium and ventricle. This allows rapid conduction between the chambers. Two types of syndrome are commonly recognised, both identified on the ECG by the presence of a slurred S wave. Type A is associated with a predominant R wave in lead V1; Type B with a predominant S wave in lead V1.

The presence of the bundle of Kent predisposes to the development of tachydysrhythmias. There is variation in the degree of conduction which occurs through the normal and abnormal channels. A poorer prognosis is indicated by the predominance of conduction through the abnormal pathway and is identified by a predominantly short P-R interval on exercise testing and 24 hr tape.

1.2

a) Infero-lateral myocardial infarction.

ST depression is seen in angina and in myocardial infarction.
Infarction is likely as ECG changes have persisted after the pain has settled and the creatine kinase is elevated at 10 hrs.

1.3

a) Hypoparathyroidism   -idiopathic
                                 -secondary to malabsorption of Mg^{++}
b) Poor compliance with medication.
   Co-existent malabsorption.
c) Ba meal and follow through examination.
   Crosby capsule biopsy.

The presence of a low calcium associated with an undetectable parathormone is likely to be due to hypoparathyroidism.
Despite adequate supplementation with calcium and vitamin D the calcium remains low, indicating either malabsorption or poor compliance. Malabsorption of magnesium may contribute as it is required as a cofactor in the synthesis of parathormone.
Barium studies will identify the presence of malabsorption in the small bowel. Pathology and bacteriology from biopsy will assist in identifying the cause.

1.4

a) The diagnosis is nephrotic syndrome.

The electrophoretic pattern indicates a low albumin, alpha-1 and gamma globulin level, a normal beta globulin, and raised alpha-2 globulin.

The plasma protein changes seen in renal impairment depend on the severity of disease. The initial abnormality is often a low albumin. The pattern shown here is that of late renal disease. Note that renal disease due to systemic lupus erythematosus can be associated with an elevated gamma globulin. A normal electrophoresis is shown in the answer to Q 8.7.

1.5

a) 1. Dilutional hyponatraemia.
   2. SIADH–secondary to a head injury or chlorpropamide therapy.
b) Serum and urine osmolality.
   Serum glucose.

The cause of the low sodium observed on day three could be due to inappropriate IV fluid replacement resulting in dilutional hyponatraemia. The syndrome of inappropriate ADH secretion may result from head injury or from the oral hypoglycaemic agent which the patient may be taking. The excess ADH results in water retention, a low serum sodium and osmolality.

1.6

a) Chronic lymphocytic leukaemia.
   Warm antibody haemolytic anaemia.
b) Reticulocyte count.
   Direct Coomb's test.
   Bone marrow aspirate.

The finding of a lymphocytosis with smear cells in an elderly patient is strongly suggestive of chronic lymphocytic leukaemia (CLL). CLL is one of the B Cell lymphoid neoplasms. The diagnosis is usually made on the finding of a lymphocytosis of greater than $10 \times 10^9/l$ with marrow infiltration of at least 40%. Lymphadenopathy and splenomegaly may be found in some patients.

A proportion of cases of CLL are complicated by the development of a warm-antibody-haemolytic anaemia. This is diagnosed by an anaemia with a high reticulocyte count and a positive direct Coomb's test.

The Coomb's test detects the presence of immunoglobulin bound to red cells in vivo. Other causes of anaemia in CLL include marrow failure (due to infiltration with lymphoid cells) and hypersplenism.

1.7

a) Intestinal malabsorption.

After a loading dose of intramuscular B_{12}, a dose of B_{12} given orally will be absorbed and excreted in the urine. In normal individuals 10% of the oral dose will be excreted in the first 24 hrs. This forms the basis of the first stage of the Schilling test, where the oral dose is radiolabelled with ^{58}Co and the i.m. dose is unlabelled.
If the percentage excretion is less than 10% this can be due to pernicious anaemia or intestinal malabsorption. These can be distinguished by repeating the oral dose along with intrinsic factor. In pernicious anaemia

the percentage excretion should be greater than 10% whereas in malabsorption it will remain less than 10%.

The results of the test can be affected by incomplete urine collection.

1.8

a) The cause of a raised CSF pressure with a high protein concentration and xanthochromia is likely to be obstruction of CSF flow. This is most likely to be due to the presence of tumour.
b) A clue to the aetiology of the CSF findings is the spontaneous clot formation, which may indicate a high fibrinogen level (a feature often associated with neoplasia).

1.9

a) Polyarteritis nodosa.
b) Biopsy of kidney.
   Anti-neutrophil cytoplasmic antibody (ANCA).

The combination of the physical findings, renal impairment with haematuria, eosinophilia and HBsAg positivity (with normal LFTs) is suggestive of polyarteritis nodosa.

Polyarteritis nodosa, which has a male predominance, is one of the vasculitides which principally involves the medium and small muscular arteries.

The kidneys are the most commonly affected organ with inflammation of the arteries leading to aneurysm formation. This results in glomerulonephritis, nephrotic syndrome and renal failure. Other organs involved include the heart, bowel and skin, the latter producing characteristic skin nodules (livido reticularis).

30% of patients show hepatitis B antigenaemia. The diagnosis of polyarteritis nodosa depends on biopsy of an affected organ – although angiography often shows aneurysmal dilatation of small vessels. Recently, raised titres of anti-neutrophil cytoplasmic antibody (ANCA) have been found in association with polyarteritis. Testing for this may assist in making the diagnosis, although ANCA is also associated with other conditions such as Wegener's granulomatosis.

1.10

a) Right-sided renal artery stenosis.

The graph shown represents the excretion of technetium-99 m labelled DTPA from both kidneys and bladder. There is a rapid rise in isotope count over the left kidney followed by a brisk fall, associated with an increasing count measured over the bladder (the thick black line on the graph). The right kidney shows delayed rise with a lower peak and delayed excretion of the isotope. This finding is characteristic of renal artery stenosis.

Renal vascular disease probably accounts for less than 5% of all patients with hypertension. It is classically associated with fibromuscular hyperplasia in the young, but in middle-aged subjects is more commonly due to atheroma. There are no specific clinical features which assist in distinguishing it from essential hypertension, although the finding of resistance to drug treatment or the presence of an abdominal bruit may be indicators of the primary cause.

Investigation is directed towards detecting the arterial lesion and assessing its importance to renal function, although no imaging technique can predict the effect on blood pressure of corrective surgery.

PAPER 2

2.1

a) Acute transmural inferior and anterior myocardial infarction is shown.
b) Complete heart block is seen on the rhythm strip.

Complete heart block is identified by complete dissociation of atrial and ventricular electrical activity.
If it occurs as a complication of inferior infarction it may be a temporary phenomenon, however, when it complicates anterior infarction it is an indication for permanent pacing.

2.2

a) Atrial fibrillation.
   Mitral stenosis.

2.3

a) Combined therapy with loop and potassium sparing diuretics.
b) Sodium depleted.

Given the history of long standing dyspnoea, the most common reason for hyponatraemia, hyperkalaemia, alkalosis and mild dehydration is combination diuretic therapy for cardiac failure.
Addison's disease may produce a similar biochemical picture.
A method of distinguishing between diuretic and Addisonian upset is revue of the biochemistry after withdrawal of diuretic treatment. If this is not possible then a normal short synacthen test will exclude Addison's disease.

2.4

a) The mode of inheritance shown is autosomal dominant.
b) The mode of inheritance shown is autosomal recessive.

2.5

Cold antibody haemolytic anaemia following mycoplasma pneumonia.

The patient's blood film shows anaemia, polychromasia and micro-spherocytes indicating that red cell damage is occurring.
This combination is suggestive of haemolysis.
The presence of autoagglutination indicates that antibodies to red blood cells are present.

The picture of a mild haemolytic anaemia in a young person (with a negative Monospot test), following a recent chest infection is very suggestive of a cold agglutination disease (CHAD) occuring after mycoplasma pneumonia.

The cold antibody production is stimulated by the infecting agent. These antibodies cross react with antigens on the red cell surface membrane and cause red cell destruction. The haemolysis is usually mild and specific treatment is not usually required.

2.6

a) The patient has acquired antibodies (inhibitor) to Factor VIII.

The development of antibodies (inhibitor) to Factor VIII occurs in about 5% of all patients with haemophilia A, and in about 10-15% of patients with previous exposure to Factor VIII. Tests for antibodies to Factor VIII are now routinely performed.

Treatment depends on the level of inhibition present and involves increasing the dose of Factor VIII, bypassing Factor VIII by the administration of Factor IX, or by the use of activated coagulation factors.

2.7

a) Gilbert's disease.
b) A 14 hr fast: a positive diagnosis can be made from a rise in bilirubin in response to this stimulus.
   Phenobarbitone treatment: leads to a reduction of elevated bilirubin.

Gilbert's disease is a harmless disorder affecting 6-10% of the population, with a male predominance. Metabolic stress results in a steep rise in serum bilirubin in affected individuals. The example shown demonstrates the effect of dehydration or fasting on the expression of the disease.

2.8

a) Pulmonary fibrosis secondary to rheumatoid arthritis.
b) Both PaO_2 and $PaCO_2$ will fall.

Resting hypoxia is shown. The low PCO_2 indicates that resting oxygenation is achieved by tachypnoea. This suggests a restrictive ventilatory defect which, given the history of arthropathy, is likely to be due to pulmonary fibrosis.

Exercise will compromise her ability to maintain oxygenation and will 'blow off' further CO_2 leading to hypocapnia.

2.9

a) Stress polycythaemia.

The finding of polycythaemia, a raised packed cell volume (PCV), normal red cell mass and reduced plasma volume is suggestive of stress polycythaemia or Gaisbock's syndrome.

The causes of this include stress, hypertension, smoking, alcohol and diuretic therapy. Treatment is by correcting the underlying cause and by venesection until the PCV is less than 0.45. This reduces the attendant risk of occlusive vascular disease.

2.10

a) Hyperprolactinaemia.
b) Amenorrhoea and galactorrhoea.
The combined anterior pituitary function testing has resulted in adequate hypoglycaemia with appropriate cortisol, GH, FSH and TSH responses. A

raised prolactin and low oestrogen are noted in the test. This indicates prolactinaemia and the low E2 shows the antigonadal effect of raised prolactin.

PAPER 3

3.1

a) Ventricular tachycardia.

The clues which help to distinguish this ECG from supraventricular tachycardia are:
   The presence of left axis deviation
   Slight variation in heart rate
   Changing conduction patterns including the presence of fusion and
   capture beats
   A-V dissociation (although this is less easily seen in this example)

3.2

a) Hyperkalaemia.

The likely cause of seizure is cerebral hypoxia or transient dysrhythmia. The feature shown is that of an aberrant broad complex ventricular rhythm.

ECG changes seen in hyperkalaemia are:
   Tented T waves
   Diminution or absence of P waves
   Broad-complex ventricular rhythm (sine wave)
   Slurring of the ST segment
   Asystole

3.3

a) A restrictive ventilatory defect.
b) Low (around 0.3 in this case).
c) The causes are the interstitial lung disorders, which, at this age and sex are likely to include sarcoidosis, systemic lupus erythematosus, and rheumatoid arthritis.
d) Rheumatoid factor
    DNA binding
    Kveim test
    Bronchoscopy with bronchoalveolar lavage and biopsy
    Chest X-ray: May vary from normal to honeycomb appearance.

Both the FEV_1 and the FVC are reduced with a FEV_1/FVC ratio of greater than 80%. These values indicate a restrictive defect and are consistent with an interstitial lung disorder.

The residual volume, estimated from the total lung capacity (TLC) and the vital capacity (FVC), is also likely to be reduced.

3.4

a) Menstrual blood loss.
    Iron deficiency related to adolescence.
    Poor diet.
b) Poor compliance with iron therapy.

The most likely cause of iron deficiency anaemia in an 18 year old girl with no medical history of note is menstrual blood loss. A normal diet contains around 15 g of iron, of which 1–1.5 mg is eventually absorbed. A menstruating female requires approximately 2.5 mg/day of iron to replace menstrual loss. In addition, iron requirements are increased during adolescence and a combination of these factors may lead to iron deficiency. The most common reason for failure of iron therapy is poor compliance with treatment.

3.5

a) Hypernatraemic dehydration.
    Pre-renal uraemia.
    Hyperosmolar non-ketotic diabetic coma.
    Urinary tract infection.
b) Serum glucose estimation.
    Serum osmolality.
    Culture of urine and blood.

Hypernatraemic dehydration is evident from the high sodium and urea and is due to predominant water loss from hyperglycaemia. The calculated osmolality from these results is 333.2 mOsmol/l, indicating a hyperosmolar state.

In this setting the renal dysfunction is likely to be secondary to dehydration (i.e. pre-renal uraemia), though pre-existing renal impairment cannot be excluded from the results given.

The presence of glycosuria may indicate a stress response but the combination of this and a hyperosmolar state in an elderly person suggests the possibilty of undiagnosed hyperosmolar non-ketotic diabetic coma.

Investigation is aimed at diagnosing underlying diabetes mellitus and excluding precipitating infection.

3.6

a) Zieve's syndrome.

The combination of haemolysis, liver impairment and hypercholesterolaemia suggests Zieve's syndrome.

Zieve's syndrome is found in alcoholic cirrhosis where hyperlipidaemia is associated with a shortening of red cell lifespan and haemolysis due to changes in the lipid component of cell membranes.

This results in an increase in red cell osmotic fragility and the presence of spherocytes in the peripheral blood.

3.7

a) Acute myeloblastic leukaemia.
b) Stage IIB Hodgkin's disease is most often treated with chemotherapy. Secondary acute myelogenous leukaemia can follow treatment with chemotherapeutic agents such as mustine and chlorambucil.

3.8

a) Turner's syndrome.
   Polycystic ovary syndrome is also associated with a high LH but a normal oestradiol level and high oestrone.
b) Chromosome analysis or buccal smear examination.
   Ultrasound of abdomen (to detect ovarian streaks).
c) Cyclical sex hormones which lead to the development of secondary sexual characteristics and menstruation.
d) None: in Turner's syndrome the girl will be infertile.

Turner's syndrome usually presents with short stature and primary amenorrhoea and is due to gonadal dysgenesis. It is associated with dysplasia or aplasia of the ovaries and results in a low oestrogen level and, by feedback, a high luteinising hormone level. It is commonly found in association with the XO chromosome abnormality.

Polycystic ovary syndrome is associated with secondary amenorrhoea, hirsutism and the presence of multiple cysts on the ovaries.

3.9

a) Familial hypertriglyceridaemia (Freidrickson's type IV).
b) Signs of hyperuricaemia and obesity.

Familial hypertriglyceridaemia is a genetic disorder often with autosomal dominant transmission. It is associated with an increase in Very Low Density Lipoprotein (VLDL) and in the risk of cardiovascular disease. It is often accompanied by hyperuricaemia, obesity and glucose intolerance.

The assignment of lipoproteins to the lipid fractionation shown in the fasting control can be explained as follows:

Alpha;	High Density Lipoprotein (HDL)
PreBeta;	Very Low Density Lipoprotein (VLDL)
Beta;	Low Density Lipoprotein (LDL)
Chylomicrons	Not seen in a fasting normal sample

Lipid abnormalities can be considered in terms of lipoprotein patterns (Freidrickson's classification) or by clinical syndromes, e.g. Familial hypercholesterolaemia, Polygenic hypercholesterolaemia etc.

3.10

a) The blood group is A_2.
b) The presence of anti A_1 antibody.

The A phenotype can be divided into various subgroups.
80% of group A individuals are classed as group A_1 and 20% as group A_2.
The phenotype A_2 is suggested by the lack of agglutination when patient's cells are tested with anti A_1 antibody.

Approximately 3% of A_2 individuals produce an antibody designated anti A_1 which reacts with A_1 cells but not A_2 cells.

PAPER 4

4.1

a) A prolonged QT interval.
b) The common causes of a prolonged QT interval are:
   Hypocalcaemia
   Myocarditis
   Ischaemic heart disease
   Quinidine toxicity.

Other causes include:
 Surdocardiac syndrome
 Romano-Ward syndrome
 Lange-Jervell-Nielsen syndrome.

The QT interval varies with the heart rate. To obtain a normal range for the QT interval a QTc is calculated.
This is obtained by dividing the QT interval by the square root of the R-R interval. The normal range for the QTc is 0.34 to 0.43 secs.

4.2

a) Right axis deviation (w + 100).
 Diminishing amplitude of R wave from V_1 to V_6.
b) Right ventricular dominance.
 Dextrocardia.

4.3

a) Serum urea and creatinine.
 Parathormone level.
b) Secondary hyperparathyroidism from chronic renal failure.

The low pCO_2 in this example suggests a metabolic acidosis being compensated by chronic hyperventilation. The presence of hyperuricaemia, hypocalcaemia and hypoalbuminaemia gives clues that this may be due to chronic renal failure. The presence of a normocytic anaemia also indicates chronicity of renal impairment.
Chronic renal failure is associated with reduced phosphate excretion and decreased metabolism of 25 hydroxyvitamin D to 1,25 dihydroxyvitamin D in the kidney. This results in hypocalcaemia.

In chronic renal failure associated with hypocalcaemia there is an appropriate increase in parathormone secretion which attempts to rectify the ionised calcium level. In secondary hyperparathyroidism plasma calcium levels are always low, or normal. However PTH secretion can become autonomous from chronic stimulation and lead to hypercalcaemia (tertiary hyperparathyroidism).

4.4

a) The presence of an atrial septal defect.
b) Two ECG patterns are associated with the presence of an ASD:

Right bundle branch block and right axis deviation (ostium secundum defect).

Right bundle branch block and left axis deviation (ostium primum defect).

The cardiac catheter studies show an increased oxygen saturation in the right atrium, implying that a communication exists between the left and right sides of the heart at this level. In addition, an increase in right atrial and ventricular pressure is seen with normal left heart pressure.

4.5

a) Disseminated intravascular coagulation (DIC).
b) Examination of the blood film for red cell fragmentation.
Estimation of fibrin degradation products (FDPs).

The features shown are suggestive of DIC secondary to a urinary tract infection.

DIC is characterised by inappropriate activation of the coagulation cascade. This leads to consumption of clotting factors, and formation of fibrin strands in microvasculature. Fragmentation of red cells and sequestration of platelets occur in the fibrin nets. Increased fibrinolysis in response to the formation of thrombin leads to the formation of FDPs.

These processes are reflected in the laboratory findings of:
A prolonged PT, PTT and TT
A depleted fibrinogen level
Thrombocytopenia
Fragmented red cells
Increased levels of FDPS.

Due to these abnormalities in the haemostatic mechanism bleeding or bruising occurs, although thrombotic episodes can also be seen.

Common causes of DIC include:

Infection: Bacterial (Gram -ve sepsis)
               Viral
Obstetric: Septic abortion
               Eclampsia
               Amniotic fluid embolus
               Ante partum haemorrhage
Malignancy: Disseminated carcinomatosis
               Leukaemia

4.6

a) A short synacthen test.
    Protein electrophoresis: to identify any paraprotein.
b) Addison's disease.
    Paraproteinaemia/Myeloma.

The abnormalities present in the data are:
    Hyponatraemia
    Mild renal impairment
    A normocytic anaemia

These features are suggestive of Addison's disease. However the presence of a high ESR requires exclusion of a paraprotein which binds sodium, produces hyponatraemia and causes an absent anion gap.

4.7

a) Allergic bronchopulmonary aspergillosis.
b) Skin test with aspergillin.
    Serum aspergillus precipitins.

The presence of eosinophilia and patchy shadowing on the X-ray in an asthmatic patient suggests the development of allergic bronchopulmonary aspergillosis.

This is an IgE mediated hypersensitivity to colonisation (not infection) by aspergillus. It is associated with an immediate-type skin reaction to aspergillus in the majority of cases and serum precipitins in 70%.

Aspergillus can colonise a pre-existing pulmonary cavity and form a mycetoma. Disseminated aspergillosis can occur in immunocompromised patients.

The 'plugs' of sputum contain eosinophils and fungi and do not indicate bacterial infection.

4.8

a) Tuberculous meningitis.
b) Ziehl Neelsen staining of the CSF for acid and alcohol fast bacilli.
   Culture of CSF for AAFB.
   Chest X-ray.
   Early morning urine collection for AAFB.

The non-specific history, the presence of a high CSF protein with a mixed cellularity response is typical of tuberculous meningitis. Similar history and findings may occur in carcinomatous involvement of the meninges. CSF cytology should be carried out to exclude this.

4.9

a) Renal glycosuria.
b) Acquired or inherited proximal tubular abnormality.
   Conditions associated with high glomerular filtration rate
   (e.g. pregnancy).

The normal renal threshold for glucose is 10 mmol/l. This is related to both renal blood flow to the proximal tubules and tubular function. In normal circumstances serum glucose does not rise above 10 mmol/l, so all glucose is reabsorbed in the proximal tubule.

Theoretically, a low glomerular filtration rate will result in more complete reabsorption of glucose at higher serum concentrations. Conversely a high

GFR, can result in glycosuria with normoglycaemia. Disturbance of tubular function (e.g. renal tubular acidosis) will also result in renal glycosuria.

4.10

a) Hereditary spherocytosis.

Osmotic fragility of red cells depends on the volume to surface area ratio of the cells and reflects their ability to take up water without lysis.

In normal red cells the biconcave shape allows the cell to increase its volume by around 70% before lysis. In the spherocytic cell the volume to surface area is increased which limits the amount of water that can be taken up before lysis.

The osmotic fragility test is carried out by incubating red cells in various concentrations of NaCl solutions and measuring the degree of lysis that occurs. If these results are plotted (percentage lysis versus concentration of NaCl solution) it can be seen that in conditions associated with spherocytosis, lysis occurs at higher concentrations of NaCl solution. This causes a shift in the fragility curve to the right and an increase in the median cell fragility (MCF). The test is carried out on cells at 20° and after incubation at 37° for 24 hrs.

A positive result can also be found in autoimmune haemolytic anaemia due to the presence of microspherocytes. This condition can usually be distinguished by its association with Coomb's test positivity.

PAPER 5

5.1

a) Wenkebach phenomenon.
b) Inferior transmural myocardial infarction.

The rhythm strip on the ECG shows a lengthening P-R interval followed by a dropped beat.

Wenkebach is a form of second degree heart block in which the atrioventricular conduction becomes progressively more delayed until there is complete block, when the atrial impulse fails to be conducted to the ventricles. It is also known as Mobitz type I block and can be a benign dysrhythmia associated with high vagal tone or, as in this case, associated with ischaemic damage to the AV node.

5.2

a) RBC folate estimation.
   Bone marrow examination.
b) Folate deficiency due to anticonvulsant therapy.

B_{12} estimation should also be performed.

Epileptic patients receiving treatment with phenytoin can develop low serum and RBC folate - a proportion going on to develop megaloblastic anaemia. The mechanism for this is unclear.

5.3

a) The limb leads have been connected incorrectly.

The limb leads show inverted P waves in lead II associated with R. axis deviation. The chest leads are normal.
The only explanation for this apparent discrepancy is that the limb leads are connected incorrectly.

5.4

a) Hypothyroidism.

The abnormalities shown include:
   hyponatraemia
   elevated creatine kinase
   a mild macrocytic anaemia
   a pleural effusion

Thyroid hormone lack is associated with a degree of inappropriate antidiuretic hormone production which may predispose to the development of hyponatraemia.

Rhabdomyolysis has also been reported with hypothyroidism and is identified on biochemical screening as an elevated creatine kinase of skeletal muscle origin.

Thyroid hormone is a cofactor for red cell production and reduced thyroid hormone levels result in the development of a macrocytic anaemia.

5.5

a) Multiple myeloma.
b) Skeletal survey.
    Electrophoresis of serum and urine.
    Bone marrow aspirate.
    Blood film: to identify rouleaux or plasma cells.

The main abnormality shown is an elevated total protein with reduction in albumin concentration (i.e. an increase in globulins). Given the clinical setting, the mild renal impairment and hypercalcaemia the most likely diagnosis is myeloma. The increase in total protein is due to paraprotein production.

The diagnosis of myeloma is made on the basis of:
    The radiological appearance of multiple lytic lesions in the bony skeleton.
    Monoclonal paraprotein in the serum, urine or both.
    Plasma cell infiltration of the bone marrow.

Other features include rouleaux formation on blood film, an increased ESR and an increase in plasma viscosity. The serum concentration of B_2 microglobulin may also be elevated, particularly if renal function is impaired.

5.6

a) Alkaline phosphatase isoenzymes.
   CT scan of head.
   Skeletal survey.
b) Paget's disease.
   Secondary carcinomatous deposits.
c) The presence of sensorineural deafness in a patient with Paget's disease is an indication for treatment with diphosphonates, even if the patient is otherwise well.

The aetiology of an isolated high alkaline phosphatase, of bone origin, in a 68 year old with recent onset sensorineural deafness suggests the possibility of Paget's disease. Secondary carcinoma should however be excluded.

The Rhinne test shows reduced air and bone conduction in the left ear. The Weber test shows deflection of hearing to the unaffected ear. This combination is suggestive of a sensorineural deafness.

CT scanning will show the presence of any space occupying lesion within the skull. Alkaline phosphatase isoenzymes will confirm it to be of bony origin. Skeletal survey will show the presence of Paget's at other sites such as skull and long bones. It will also show any skeletal secondary carcinomatous deposits.

5.7

a) Metabolic acidosis.
   Thiamine deficiency.

Measurement of red blood cell transketolase activity is a sensitive indicator of thiamine deficiency as this enzyme is dependent on thiamine pyrophosphate (TPP) as a cofactor.

An increase of more than 10% in transketolase activity in the patient's red cells with the addition of TPP indicates thiamine deficiency.

Thiamine deficiency in Western countries occurs almost exclusively in chronic alcoholics whose diet is deficient in the vitamin. Thiamine is necessary for the decarboxylation of pyruvate. In conditions of deficiency, pyruvate and lactate accumulate causing a metabolic acidosis.

5.8

a) Cyclical neutropenia.

Episodes of neutropenia alternating with a normal neutrophil count on a regular basis suggests cyclical neutropenia. The most common period of oscillation is 19–21 days. The disorder presents as episodic infections, especially of the skin. The finding of fever and oral ulceration are also characteristic. The disease is thought to be familial.

5.9

a) Chest X-ray.
   Blood,urine and stool cultures.
   Legionella titres.
b) Septicaemia/UTI.
   Legionellosis.

The appearance of fever, leucocytosis and hypoxia may be due to septicaemia consequent upon a urinary tract infection.
However the combination of confusion, diarrhoea and hyponatraemia should lead one to suspect Legionnaire's disease.

5.10

a) Irreversible airways obstruction.

From the graph a number of parameters of airway physiology can be calculated.
The FEV_1 is calculated from the air flow found at one second (approximately 0.8l).
The FVC is calculated from the air flow found at seven seconds (approximately 2.5l).

The ratio of FEV_1/FVC can then be calculated (0.8/2.5, which equals 0.32 or 32%).

This indicates severe airways obstruction post-bronchodilator therapy and likely irreversible airways obstruction.

The normal FEV_1/FVC ratio is 75%.
Reduced FEV_1 and FVC with a normal ratio indicates a restrictive ventilatory defect.
Reduced FEV_1 and FVC with a reduced ratio indicates an obstructive ventilatory defect.

PAPER 6

6.1

a) Supraventricular tachycardia.
   Right bundle branch block.
b) In the presence of shock, electrical or pharmacological cardioversion is required.

6.2

a) The two main diagnoses evident on the ECG are:
   Slow atrial fibrillation.
   Inferior myocardial infarction.

In addition, reciprocal ischaemic changes are seen in the lateral chest leads.

6.3

a) Acute myeloblastic leukaemia.

Acute myeloblastic leukaemia accounts for 80% of adult acute leukaemias. Peripheral blood counts may show a raised white cell count, but often the white count, haemoglobin concentration and platelet counts are low.

Cytochemistry is of use in determining whether an acute leukaemia is lymphoblastic or myeloblastic and is of particular value when morphology of the marrow does not assist in classification.

Typical patterns of cytochemistry for acute myeloblastic leukaemia (AML), acute lymphoblastic leukaemia (ALL), and acute monocytic leukaemia (AMoL) are shown below:

	Myeloperoxidase	*Sudan Black*	*PAS*	*Non-spec Esterase*
A M L	+ +	+ +	-	-
A L L	-	-	+ +	-
A Mo L	+ +	+ +	-	+ +

6.4

a) X-linked recessive inheritance.
b) Duchenne muscular dystrophy.
   Haemophilia.

The pedigree shows a condition that affects only males and does not occur in every generation. The affected male transmits the recessive gene to all of his daughters and none of his sons.
A daughter is not affected as the abnormal gene is masked by a normal X chromosome. She is however a carrier, being heterozygous for the affected X chromosome. Such a female has a one in two chance of transmitting the affected gene to her sons, who will then be affected by the condition. She also has a one in two chance of passing the affected gene to her daughters, who would then be carriers of the condition.

Apart from the conditions mentioned above, a number of other conditions show an X-linked inheritance:
   Glucose 6 phosphate dehydrogenase deficiency
   Lesch-Nyhan syndrome
   Hunter's syndrome
   Red-green colour blindness.

6.5

a) Inadequate cortisol response to insulin due to failure to induce adequate hypoglycamia.
b) A Synacthen test should be carried out to exclude a primary failure of cortisol secretion.
c) If a Synacthen test is normal the diagnosis is that of insulin resistance.

Before analysing the results of anterior pituitary stimulation tests it is important to ensure that adequate hypoglycaemia has been acheived (glucose 2 mmol/l) and that the hypoglycaemia results in a rise in cortisol level by 220 nmol/l to a value greater than 550 nmol/l.

The dose of insulin given in the question represents double the dose used in the standard test. Despite this, adequate hypoglycaemia has not been achieved. This suggests that there may be an excessive quantitiy of antagonists to insulin present.

This may occur in acromegaly where there is an excess of circulating growth hormone.

6.6

a) Ferritin estimation to exclude iron deficiency.
   Family history.
b) Sickle thalassaemia.
   Sickle cell anaemia.

From the data given the relevant abnormalities are:
   A normal haemoglobin and a low MCV
   Absent HbA
   High HbS and HbF.

The most likely diagnosis from this combination is Sickle/Thalassaemia. Sickle cell anaemia is a possibility, though 25% HbF is unusually high for this diagnosis. Hereditary persistence of fetal haemoglobin (HPFH) is associated with a high HbF, so Sickle/HPFH is a third, but rarer, possibility.

6.7

a) Cutaneous hepatic porphyria.
b) Venesection may relieve symptoms.
The porphyrias are caused by an acquired or inherited deficiency of one of the enzymes required for haem synthesis.
This results in impaired haem synthesis and overproduction of haem precursors (the porphyrins).

The features of this group of disorders include the development of a photosensitive skin rash (when circulating porphyrins are increased) and neurological manifestations such as neuritis and abdominal pain. Neurological disturbance usually occurs when porphobilinogen and delta-aminolaevulinic acid are produced in excess.

Excessive haem production occurs either in the liver (the hepatic porphyrias) or in the erythropoetic system (the erythropoetic porphyrias). Further discussion of the mechanism of these disorders is beyond the scope of this book, however the table below describes a basic guide to distinguishing the chronic porphyrias, associated with skin lesions, on the basis of biochemical findings.

Associated with neurological disturbance in acute attacks

	Urine dALA/PBG	*Urine porphyrins*	*Faeces porphyrins*
Porphyria variegata	- (+)	- (+)	+ (+)
Hereditary coproporphyria	- (+)	- (+)	+ (+)

Not associated with neurological manifestations

Cutaneous hepatic porphyria	-	+	-
Congenital erythropoetic porphyria	-	+	+
Erythrohepatic porphyria	-	-	+

Figures in brackets indicate acute attacks.

NB   Hereditary coproporphyria is rarely associated with skin lesions.

6.8

a) Metabolic acidosis.
   Normal anion gap.
   Hyperchloraemia.
   Hyponatraemia.
   Hypokalaemia.
   Elevated creatinine.
b) The most likely cause from the history given is that of a ureteric diversion.

With any change in acid-base balance, electrical neutralilty must be preserved. In a normal individual the majority of extracellular anions are chloride and bicarbonate. Sodium and potassium account for the majority of cations. The anion gap is the difference between cations and anions and is expressed in milliequivalents.
i.e. $(Na^+ + K^+) - (HCO3^- + Cl^-)$ = the anion gap.

The anion gap represents anions not routinely estimated (e.g. proteins, urate, phosphate, sulphate) in normal circumstances. Ketoacids, lactic acid and salicylate excesses will be revealed as an increase in the anion gap in the relevant disease states.

In the example shown, the anion gap is within normal limits as the acidosis is due to excess chloride which is accounted for in the anion gap equation.

The differential diagnosis of an acidosis with a normal anion gap includes:
   Acetazolamide therapy
   Renal tubular acidosis
   Ammonium chloride administration
   Ureteric transplantation.

6.9

a) Lead poisoning.
b) Urinary delta-amino laevulinic acid levels.
   Urinary coproporphyrin levels.

The finding of a mildly hypochromic anaemia accompanied by punctate basophilia is suggestive of a diagnosis of lead poisoning. Punctate basophilia is due to precipitated DNA and occurs mainly in lead poisoning although it can also be found in other haemolytic conditions (e.g. leukaemia and some haemoglobinopathies).

Lead impairs haem synthesis and causes increased urinary excretion of delta amino laevulinic acid and coproporphyrin.

6.10

a) A metabolic acidosis with a high anion gap (22.1 meq/l).
   Hypoglycaemia.
   The presence of an osmotically active substance producing a difference between calculated and measured osmolality of 38.5 mmol/l.
   A high creatinine accompanied by a normal urea.
b) Alcohol excess in a chronic alcoholic.

Alcohol excess can induce hypoglycaemia by suppression of hepatic gluconeogenesis. The metabolic acidosis may be due to a combination of renal impairment and ketoacidosis (as a result of vomiting). The clue to the diagnosis is the presence of an osmotically active substance in the blood not accounted for in the calculation of serum osmolality. The commonest cause of this is alcohol.

The normal urea despite an elevated creatinine suggests that chronic liver impairment has resulted in decreased urea production. Approximate serum osmolality is obtained by adding the concentration of the following elements (expressed in mmol/l):

$$(2 \times Na^+) + (2 \times K^+) + Urea + Glucose$$

The result is expressed in mOsmol/l or mmol/l.

PAPER 7

7.1

a) Ventricular trigemini.
    Complete left bundle branch block.

7.2

a) Ferritin estimation.
    Liver biopsy.
b) Haemochromatosis.
    Iron overload secondary to alcoholism.

Haemochromatosis is suggested by the features of hepatomegaly, mild derangement of LFTs, diabetes and excessive serum iron.

The disease is inherited as an autosomal trait and the diagnosis is made by demonstrating excess parenchymal iron. Ferritin is generally considered to be a better measure of total body iron stores than serum iron. Measurement of urinary excretion of iron following desferrioxamine therapy is also useful in establishing the diagnosis of iron overload.
Alcoholics with cirrhosis may also develop iron overload in the liver. In these circumstances total body iron stores are usually less than in haemochromatosis and there is evidence of greater hepatic dysfunction. Diabetes in this situation is uncommon.

7.3

a) Anterior myocardial infarction.
    Ventricular aneurysm.

Ventricular aneurysm is less likely as pathological Q waves are not seen and the axis is normal.

7.4

a) Contamination of the venous sample with heparin.

Umbilical vein catheters are used in neonates to provide venous access for blood sampling and are flushed with a heparin based solution to maintain patency. If the initial sample from these lines is not discarded then heparin contamination of the sample will affect the coagulation screen leading to gross prolongation of the prothrombin and partial thromboplastin times.

A similar situation occurs, in adults, when samples are taken from indwelling venous or arterial catheters, or are of insufficient volume relative to the anticoagulant containers used for coagulation screen estimation.

7.5

a) Urea and creatinine estimation.
   Calculation of calcium corrected for albumin.
   X-rays of spine and pelvis.
   Ferritin estimation.
b) Dehydration.

The presence of a high haematocrit accompanied by a proportional increase in globulins, total protein and albumin suggest the diagnosis of dehydration. The presence of a raised alkaline phosphatase may indicate the presence of a fracture.

A low mean corpuscular volume suggests that iron deficiency or failure of iron utilisation is present.

In the example given the corrected calcium was obtained from the following formula:

$$Ca^{++}(adj) = Ca^{++}(tot) + (47\text{-Albumin})$$

NB Different laboratories use different standard albumin concentrations for this calculation

7.6

a) Fasting cholesterol fractionation.
   Exclusion of myocardial infarction.
b) Hypercholesterolaemia.
   Congenital deficiency of thyroid binding globulin (TBG).

The data reveals a low total T_4, with normal T_3, free T_4 and TSH. This implies that the level of TBG is low as the free fractions are normal. The patient is euthyroid.

Hypercholesterolaemia should make one consider hypothyroidism or nephrotic syndrome. However, hypothyroidism would be associated with a raised TSH and low free T_4. Nephrotic syndrome is an unlikely cause of the low TBG as total protein, globulins and, by inference, albumin, are normal.

Causes of a low TBG:
   Neprotic syndrome
   Congenital deficiency of TBG.

Causes of a raised TBG:
   Pregnancy
   Newborn
   Use of the combined oral contraceptive pill.

7.7

a) A rise in acid concentration of greater than 20 meq/l over the basal level.
   This indicates an incomplete vagotomy.

Insulin induced hypoglycaemia stimulates gastric acid secretion via the vagus nerve. A complete vagotomy should result in a flat response of acid secretion to the effects of hypoglyaemia.

7.8

a) Hairy cell leukaemia.

Hairy cell leukaemia is one of the B-lymphoproliferative disorders that predominantly affects middle-aged males. Splenomegaly is the most common clinical finding, often accompanied by hepatomegaly. Lymphadenopathy is rare.

Laboratory findings are those of a pancytopenia and the presence of hairy cells in the peripheral blood. Hairy cells resemble lymphocytes but are much larger and have abundant cytoplasm that is villous in appearance.

Tartrate resistant acid phosphatase in hairy cells is specific for the disease.

7.9

a) Aortic outflow obstruction/aortic stenosis.
b) None. Surgery is indicated if the pressure gradient between the left ventricle and the systolic blood pressure exceeds 50 mmHg.

There is a difference in the systolic blood pressure and the left ventricular systolic pressure of 45 mmHg. This is consistent with obstruction at the aortic outflow and is likely to be due to aortic stenosis. The other pressures and cardiac output remain within normal limits.

7.10

a) Serum antinuclear factor and rheumatoid factor.
   Blood glucose and amylase estimation.
b) Rheumatoid arthritis related pleural effusion.

<u>PAPER 8</u>

8.1

A high nodal rhythm with retrograde conduction to the atria.

An incomplete left bundle branch block is also seen.

8.2

a) Left axis deviation and right bundle branch block (i.e. bifasicular block)
b) Bifasicular block is an indication for insertion of a permanent pacemaker.

8.3

a) Intravascular haemolytic anaemia.
b) Salazopyrin therapy.

Salazopyrin can cause intravascular haemolytic anaemia.
The blood film shows the features of haemolysis (spherocytes, polychromasia and fragmented red cells).
Haemosiderin derived from red cell breakdown can be found in the urine in severe cases.

Similar drug induced haemolysis is found with:
  Dapsone
  Maloprim
  Nitrates
  Nitrites

8.4

a) Blood glucose estimation.
  Electrocardiograph.
b) Stress hyperglycaemia.
  New onset diabetes mellitus.
  Renal glycosuria.

The likely diagnosis of glycosuria in the presence of a normal HbA$_{1c}$ is stress hyperglycaemia. Glucose homeostasis can be upset by the physiological secretion, during stress, of chemicals which have a hyperglycaemic action. These include the glucocorticoids and adrenaline.

From the data given, a reduction in the renal threshold (normally 10 mmol/l) for glucose cannot be excluded. The presence of such a tubular defect would cause glycosuria in the presence of normal blood glucose levels.

8.5

a) Ultrasound of abdomen.
   Erythropoietin level.
b) Conditions associated with inappropriate secretion of erythropoietin:
   Hypernephroma (renal carcinoma).
   Hepatoma.
   Cerebellar haemangioma.
   Uterine fibroid.

In this case there is an increased red cell mass, normal arterial pO$_2$, and normal bone marrow.

The normal arterial pO$_2$ excludes hypoxia-induced (appropriate) polycythaemia. A normal bone marrow examination excludes a primary myeloproliferative disorder.

8.6

a) Serum glucose.
   Arterial blood gases.
   Salicylate levels.
b) Diabetic keto- or lactic acidosis with a coagulopathy.
   Salicylate overdose.
   Stress hyperglycaemia due to dehydration.

In salicylate overdose both hyper and hypoglycaemia can occur.
The typical pattern is of hypoglycaemia accompanied by a reducing substance (salicylate) in the urine. The other features in the data given

represent the metabolic response to the accompanying acidosis and dehydration.

Salicylates initially lead to a respiratory alkalosis by direct stimulation of the respiratory centre. In higher dosage they impair aerobic metabolism and cause a lactic acidosis.

A combination of these effects leads to a variety of pH changes depending on which abnormality predominates.

8.7

a) Bone marrow trephine.
   Neutrophil (Leucocyte) alkaline phosphatase score.
   Bone marrow chromosomal analysis for the presence of the Philadelphia chromosome.
b) A leucoerythroblastic anaemia.
   Chronic myelogenous leukaemia (CML).

The features of anaemia accompanied by nucleated red cells and white cell precursors in the peripheral blood is suggestive of a leucoerythroblastic anaemia.

These features could also be accounted for by chronic myelogenous leukaemia. In both cases, although marrow aspirate can be successful, a trephine is usually required to indicate the cause of a leucoerythroblastic anaemia and to demonstrate the presence of CML.

The Philadelphia chromosome may be present in CML.
The neutrophil alkaline phosphatase scores will be low in CML and raised in a leucoerythroblastic anaemia.

Causes of a leucoerythroblastic anaemia include:
   Metastatic involvement of the marrow by carcinoma (commonly prostatic, breast or lung)
   Myelofibrosis
   Myeloma
   Severe haemorrhage or haemolysis.

8.8

a) A proportional increase in all protein fractions.
b) Dehydration.
   Prolonged use of a tourniquet during sampling.

The illustration below shows a normal electrophoretic pattern.

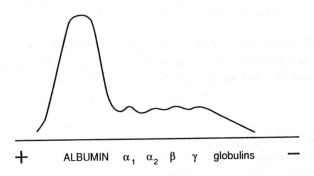

Changes in protein electrophoresis	Cause
Albumin low	Any illness
Albumin low, α-1 and 2 increased	Acute phase reaction
Albumin low, gamma diffusely increased	Autoimmune diseases
Albumin low, α-1 low, gamma increased with apparent β-Gamma fusion	Cirrhosis
Albumin low, α-1 and gamma low, α-2 increased	Nephrotic syndrome

NB These patterns, although typical, are not diagnostic of the conditions shown.

8.9

a) Lymph node biopsy.
b) Lymphoma.

The Monospot test detects the heterophile antibody produced in infectious mononucleosis and is usually sensitive and specific for the disease.

In this example the Monospot is positive whilst the IgG and IgM titres are negative. This suggests a false positive Monospot test.

False positive tests are found in association with lymphoma and hepatitis. In this case the presence of lymphadenopathy suggests the diagnosis of lymphoma and a lymph node biopsy should be carried out.

8.10

a) Increased creatinine clearance.
b) Early diabetes mellitus nephropathy.

An increased creatinine clearance is occasionally seen in early diabetic nephropathy due to increased filtration.

The creatinine clearance can be calculated as follows:

$$\frac{(\text{Creatinine concentration})_{urine} \times \text{Urine output}}{(\text{Creatinine concentration})_{serum}}$$

*concentrations are expressed in mmol/ml
*urine output in ml/min

The figures for Q 8.10 are:

$$\frac{7.8 \text{ mmol/l} \times 1440/(60 \times 24) \text{ ml/min}}{0.060 \text{ mmol/l}}$$

Creatinine clearance = 130 ml/min

PAPER 9

9.1

a) Atrial fibrillation.
   Left bundle branch block.

9.2

a) Primary biliary cirrhosis.
   Chronic hepatitides.
b) Hepatitis B surface antigen estimation.
   Anti nuclear factor estimation.
   Liver biopsy.

The data reveal an elevated caeruloplasmin level and an increased urinary copper.

Caeruloplasmin is an α_2-globulin, and a raised level is found as part of an acute phase reaction to tissue damage. A raised level is also commonly found in acute hepatic upset and in chronic liver disease, especially when associated with biliary obstruction. Occasionally elevated levels are found in pregnancy or with use of the oral contraceptive pill.

An elevated urinary copper estimation is seen in Wilson's disease, where it often exceeds 100 μg/day, but is also found in other chronic hepatic disorders. Wilson's disease is universally associated with a reduced or normal caeruloplasmin level.

9.3

a) A wandering atrial pacemaker.

The rhythm strip shows a progressively altering P wave.
Initially inverted, it becomes upright as the P-R interval lengthens.
This is usually a benign condition.

9.4

a) Pituitary driven cortisol excess.
   Obesity.
   Stress.
   Alcoholism.

The data reveal a moderately raised urinary free cortisol.
This fails to be suppressed to less than 75% of Day 1 value by low dose dexamethasone. This implies that either the feedback centre in the pituitary is insensitive to the levels of cortisol, or that maximal negative feedback is already present.

High dose dexamethasone succeeds in suppressing the baseline figure to less than 50%, suggesting that the underlying diagnosis is an insensitive pituitary gland. This results in excessive ACTH and, by stimulation of the adrenal cortex, excess cortisol.

Such a pattern is found in pituitary driven excess cortisol (Cushing's disease).

Occasionally failure of low dose dexamethasone suppression is seen in obesity, excess stress, or severe alcoholism. This is usually suppressed by the high dose dexamethasone and can cause diagnostic confusion.

Dexamethasone suppression responses in excess cortisol is shown below.

Aetiology	*Cx Plasma*	*Cx Urine*	*2 mg Dex*	*8 mg Dex*	*ACTH*
Pituitary driven	N/High	High	No Supp	Supp	N/High
Ectopic ACTH	High	V High	No Supp	No Supp	V High
Adrenal carcinoma	High	V High	No Supp	No Supp	Low
Adrenal adenoma	N/High	High	No Supp	No Supp	Low

Cx = Cortisol
Dex = Dexamethasone

9.5

a) Emphysema.

The graph shows a total lung capacity (TLC) of approximately 6.2 litres, a residual volume (RV) of 2 litres and a peak expiratory flow rate (PEFR) of 2.8 litres/sec.
This indicates a raised TLC and RV with a reduced PEFR, which is consistent with pulmonary emphysema.

Lung function test patterns

	PEFR	RV	TLC	FEV$_1$ Resp to B agonist
Asthma	↓↓	↑↑	↑	> 20%
Emphysema	↓	↓↓	↑↑	< 20%
Fibrosis	N/↓	↓	↓↓	0

Key
↓   = Reduced
↓↓ = Much reduced
↑   = Increased
↑↑ = Much increased
N   = Normal
0   = No response

9.6

a) Group O.
b) Lack of expected anti-A and anti-B haemagglutinins.

The blood group is O as there is no agglutination of the patient's red cells when tested with anti-A and anti-B antibodies.

However a patient with blood group O should be expected to have naturally occuring anti-A and anti-B antibodies. These will react with test cells. This is not seen in the data shown and is due to the lack of anti-A and anti-B in serum.

Impaired anti-A and anti-B activity occur in:
Infants – as anti-A and anti-B activity is not fully evident until six months of age.
Congenital or acquired hypogammaglobulinaemia – leading to an absence of red cell agglutinins

N.B. When faced with a blood grouping question ensure that the control panel is present and has worked.

9.7

a) A dimorphic blood film.
   Hyposplenism.
b) Coeliac disease.
The presence of microcytes and macrocytes suggests concomitant deficiency of iron and B12 and/or folate, resulting in a dimorphic blood film.

Additionally, the features of hyposplenism are present. These include target cells, Howell-Jolly bodies and irregularly contracted red blood cells.

Given the clinical history of weight loss and diarrhoea, coeliac disease with splenic atrophy is the most likely diagnosis.

Other causes of a dimorphic film include:
Iron deficiency on treatment
Myelodysplasia

9.8

a) The presence of a lupus anticoagulant.

The combination of a thrombotic episode and a prolonged partial thromboplastin time suggests the presence of lupus anticoagulant activity.

This occurs relatively frequently in patients with systemic lupus erythematosus but can occur in other collagen-vascular disorders.

Lupus anticoagulant inhibits Factor X activation but paradoxically is associated with episodes of thrombosis rather than haemorrhage.

9.9

a) Blood film examination.
   Coagulation screening.
   Fibrin degradation product estimation.
b) Haemolytic-uraemic syndrome.

Haemolytic-uraemic syndrome affects all ages, but predominantly children. It is associated with features of intravascular haemolysis along with uraemia.

Examination of the blood film shows features of disseminated intravascular coagulation and the coagulation screen is frequently deranged. Fibrin degradation products may be increased.

A number of aetiologies have been identified including viral infection and some bacteria (particularly *Escherichia coli* 0157).

9.10

a) Failure of urinary concentration.
   Urinary concentration with desmopressin.
   Greater than 8% weight loss at 8 hrs.
b) Complete cranial diabetes insipidus.

There is no rise in urine osmolality in response to an increase in plasma osmolality. After desmopressin is administered urine osmolality rises. This implies that the renal response to vasopressin (anti-diuretic hormone) is intact and that there is failure of production/secretion of vasopressin by the hypothalamus/pituitary unit.

A normal response to water deprivation would be an increase in urine osmolality to 600 mOsm/kg at the end of the test. If greater than 8% weight loss occurs during the test it should be terminated.

PAPER 10

10.1

a) Atrial flutter.
   Complete heart block.
   Antero-lateral ST-T changes.

10.2

a) Pulmonary hypertension.

P Pulmonale is diagnosed when the P wave is peaked and is greater than 2.5mm tall.
It indicates right atrial hypertrophy and/or enlargement, and is usually consequent upon pulmonary hypertension.

10.3

a) Platelet and white blood cell counts.
b) Pseudohyperkalaemia as found in:
   Acute myeloproliferative disorders
   Chronic myeloproliferative disorders
   Chronic lymphatic leukaemia
   Rheumatoid arthritis.

Pseudohyperkalaemia is caused by lysis of leucocytes or platelets during venepuncture or separation of serum. It occurs in conditions associated with high platelet or WBC counts.

The correct diagnosis can be made by collection of samples using a large bore needle or by processing plasma (as opposed to serum) or heparinised samples.

10.4

a) Shortening of the partial thromboplastin time.
b) Recent deep venous thrombosis/Pulmonary thromboembolism.
   Difficulty/delay in venepuncture.
   Post partum.
c) Repeat the analysis in the first instance.

Shortening of the PTT may be an indicator of a pro-thrombotic state, and it has been reported in a number of conditions.

The PTT is particularly sensitive to tissue clotting factors resulting from a difficult venepuncture. On obtaining a shortened PTT result, repeat the test with a fresh venepuncture.

Other causes of a shortened PTT include:
   Exercise
   Post-operative
   Oestrogen therapy
   Pregnancy

10.5

a) A T cell lymphocytosis is evident.
   There is a reversed CD4/CD8 ratio.
   A positive monospot.
b) Infection with Epstein-Barr virus.

The principle of this question is to identify the cells as T cells and to note that the majority are marking as suppressor cells (CD8). A suppressor cell lymphocytosis is seen in response to viral infections, such as CMV, EBV and HIV.

The combination of CD2, CD8, and CD56 positive cells suggests that these are, in fact, natural killer cells. It is unlikely that candidates for the MRCP examination would be expected to make this interpretation of the results.

10.6

a) Bilateral sensorineural deafness.
b) Congenital rubella.

A normal audiogram is shown below.

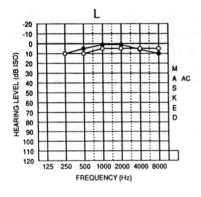 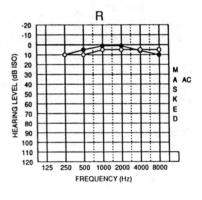

10.7

a) T3 Thyrotoxicosis.

This lady presents with the clinical features of hyperthyroidism with a normal T4 result. The TSH level is low suggesting suppression of secretion. This combination of features is suggestive of T3 thyrotoxicosis.

T3 thyrotoxicosis accounts for between 5-10% of all cases of thyrotoxicosis worldwide, but in the U.K., this falls to approximately 1% of cases.

10.8

a) Culture of ascitic fluid.
b) Immediate commencement of broad-spectrum antimicrobial therapy.

Ascites occuring in cirrhosis can be associated with infection.
Common organisms include *Escherichia coli* and pneumococci.
Fever may be a manifestation, though occasionally there are no specific clinical signs present.

If a deterioration occurs in the clinical condition of a patient with ascites, infection should be suspected. Cell counts of $350/mm^3$ with 30% neutrophils in ascitic fluid are suggestive of infection.

Treatment should be commenced without awaiting culture results as this condition is associated with a high mortality.

10.9

a) The preoperative blood group is O.
    The postoperative blood group is A.
b) The samples have been taken from two different patients.

The most common cause of discrepancies in ABO grouping is clerical error, either with sampling or labelling of specimens.

10.10

a) Reticulocyte count.
    Examination of urinary sediment for haemosiderin.
    Ham's acid lysis test.
b) Paroxysmal nocturnal haemoglobinuria (PNH).

The diagnosis of PNH is suggested by the presentation, in a young man, of abdominal pain and a vascular occlusion.

The data shown reveals evidence of haemolysis (a high lactate dehydrogenase), discolouration of urine and pancytopenia. Further investigations should establish a diagnosis of intravascular haemolysis by reticulocyte count and examination of the urine for urinary haemosiderin.

The diagnosis of PNH is confirmed by the demonstration of unusual sensitivity of the patient's red cells to haemolysis by normal complement: a positive Ham's acid lysis test.

Very few other causes of haemolysis are associated with major intravascular thrombosis.

PasTest Intensive Revision Courses

PasTest are specialists in postgraduate medical education with over 21 years of experience. We can help you to pass your exams first time with our range of books and intensive revision courses. Courses are held at convenient venues in London and Manchester. Past exam questions and favourite exam topics are discussed and analysed together with advice on exam technique. High quality teaching notes and practice exams are included. The pass rates for candidates who have attended PasTest courses is excellent.

We cover the following examinations:

MRCP Part 1 (General Medicine and Paediatrics)
MRCP Part 2 (General Medicine, Paediatrics and Clinicals)
MRCGP, DRCOG, MRCOG, DCH, FRCS, FRCA and PLAB.

For full details about our range of books and courses please contact PasTest on 01565 755226 or post the form below to

PasTest, Dept. DI, Egerton Court, Parkgate Estate, Knutsford, Cheshire, WA16 8DX

- -

Order Form

Please send me details of PasTest books and courses for

....(exam)

Name: .... Post held:....................

Address: ....

.... Telephone: ....

PasTest, Dept. DI, Egerton Court, Parkgate Estate, Knutsford, Cheshire, WA16 8DX

REVISION INDEX

A
Acidosis
  compensated metabolic, 1
  hyperchloraemic, 8
  metabolic, 1,74, 153
Addisons disease, 62, 148
ADH, 134
Anaemia
  haemolytic, 15, 103, 135, 165
  iron deficiency, 49, 142
  sickle cell anaemia, 84, 157
Ascites, 129, 178
Aspergillosis, 63, 148
Asthma, 63, 148
Audiogram, 128, 177
Autoagglutination
  cold, 4, 37, 139

B
Blood film
  dimorphic, 6
  leucoerythroblastic, 2, 167
  punctate basophilia, 14, 87, 160
Blood gases, 40, 140
Blood grouping, 54, 117, 130, 145, 172, 178
Blood volume studies, 40, 140

C
Calcium
hypercalcaemia, 72, 152
  hypocalcaemia, 24, 134
Caeruloplasmin, 113, 170
Cardiac catheter, 60, 97, 147, 164
Cell markers, 127, 176
Cerebrospinal fluid, 3
Chlorpropamide, 134
Cirrhosis, 113, 170
Coagulation,
  disseminated intravascular, 4, 61, 147
Coeliac disease, 118, 173
Copper, 113, 170
Cortisol, 41, 115, 140, 170
Creatine kinase, 67, 192
Cyclical neutropaenia, 74, 154
Cytochemistry, 5, 81, 155

D
Dapsone, 165
Dehydration, 50, 94, 108, 143, 162, 168
Dexamethasone suppression test, 6, 115, 171

Diabetes
  hyperosmolar, 50, 143
  insipidus, 18, 120, 174
  mellitus, 110, 169
Drug compliance, 49, 142

E
Electrocardiograph
  atrial flutter, 123, 175
  atrial fibrillation, 35, 81, 113, 138, 155, 170
  dextrocardia, 59, 146
  heart block
    -bifasicular, 103, 165
    -complete, 33, 123, 138, 175
    -left bundle branch
      complete, 91, 113, 161, 170
      incomplete, 101, 165
    -right bundle branch, 79, 155
  hyperkalaemia, 7, 47, 141
  lead placement, 71, 151
  myocardial infarction
    -anterior, 33, 93, 138, 161
    -inferior, 23, 33, 69, 81, 133, 138, 150, 155
  nodal rhythm, 101, 165
  p pulmonale, 125, 175
  right axis deviation, 59, 146
  QT prolongation, 57, 145
  ventricular aneurysm, 93, 161
  ventricular tachycardia, 7, 45, 141
  ventricular trigemini, 91, 161
  wandering atrial pacemaker, 115, 170
  Wenkebach phenomenon, 69, 150
  Wolf-Parkinson-White syndrome
    (type B), 20, 133
Electrophoresis
  protein, 13
Emphysema, 116, 172
Eosinophilia, 29, 136
Erythropoeitin, 7, 105, 166

F
Folate, 69, 151

G
Gaisbock's syndrome, 40, 140
Genetic pedigree, 8, 36, 82, 138, 156
Gilberts disease, 39, 139
Glucose
  hyperglycaemia, 104, 165
  tolerance test, 65, 149
Glycosuria, 149